Emblem of the
Virgin Mary

Eyewitness
MEDIEVAL
LIFE

Medieval badge
of Christ

Written by
ANDREW LANGLEY

Photographed by
GEOFF BRIGHTLING & GEOFF DANN

Trestle table

Dorling Kindersley

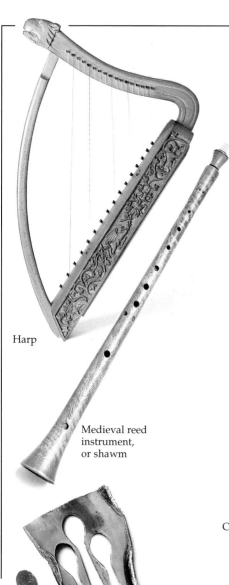

Harp

Medieval reed
instrument,
or shawm

Spoons
cut from
horn

Decorated
ceramic jugs
for wine or ale

LONDON, NEW YORK, MUNICH,
MELBOURNE, and DELHI

Project editor Bridget Hopkinson
Art editor Vicky Wharton
Designer Kati Poynor
Managing editor Gillian Denton
Managing art editor Julia Harris
Researcher Céline Carez
Production Charlotte Trail
Picture research Kathy Lockley
Consultants Peter Brears & Charles Kightly

PAPERBACK EDITION
Managing editor Andrew Macintyre
Managing art editor Jane Thomas
Editor and reference compiler Lorrie Mack
Art editor Rebecca Johns
Production Jenny Jacoby
Picture research Sarah Pownall
DTP designer Siu Yin Ho

4 6 8 10 9 7 5 3

This Eyewitness ® Guide has been conceived by
Dorling Kindersley Limited and Editions Gallimard

Hardback edition first published in Great Britain in 1996.
This edition published in Great Britain in 2002
by Dorling Kindersley Limited,
80 Strand, London WC2R ORL

A CIP catalogue record for this book is
available from the British Library.

ISBN 0 7513 4747 7

Colour reproduction by
Colourscan, Singapore
Printed in Hong Kong by Toppan

See our complete
catalogue at

www.dk.com

Stone carving of a man
"pulling a face"

"Back" stool

Drinking
vessel

Table setting

Wooden
food
bowl

Eyewitness

MEDIEVAL
LIFE

Pater noster qui es in caelis ✢
Sanctificetur nomen tuum ✢
Adveniat regnum tuum ✢
Fiat voluntas tuas sicut in
caelo et in terra ✢ Panem
nostrum quotidianum da nobis
hodie ✢ Et dimitte nobis de-
bita nostra sicut et nos dim-
ittimus debitoribus nostris ✢
Et ne nos inducas in temp-
tatione ✢ Sed libera nos
a malo ✢ Amen ✢

Horn book

Writing quills

Horn inkwells

Papal ring

Carved wooden
angel from
a medieval
church nave

Church
censer for
burning
incense

Medieval stone
carving of a
woman's head

Shepherd's
horn pipe

12th-century
reliquary casket

Bagpipes

Contents

Tester bed

The Middle Ages

The term "medieval" comes from the Latin *medium aevum*, which means "the middle ages". But when were the Middle Ages? Before them came the Classical Age of Ancient Greece and Rome, and after came the Renaissance (p. 62). The Middle Ages covered the period roughly in between, from the fifth century to the end of the 15th. In many ways medieval times seem remote and mysterious, peopled by knights and ladies, kings and bishops, monks and pilgrims. Yet European cities, states, parliaments, banking systems, and universities all have their roots there, and parts of the landscape are still dominated by the great medieval castles and cathedrals.

A LIGHT IN THE DARK
During the Dark Ages, art and learning survived in remote monasteries. This illuminated letter comes from the Book of Kells (c. 800), which was kept at St Columba's monastery in Ireland.

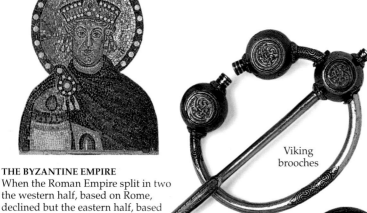

THE BYZANTINE EMPIRE
When the Roman Empire split in two the western half, based on Rome, declined but the eastern half, based on the Byzantine capital of Constantinople (now Istanbul), flourished. Its greatest ruler was the Christian emperor Justinian I (c. 482–565).

Viking brooches

SEA RAIDERS
The Vikings began to raid the coasts of Europe towards the end of the eighth century.

KING OF EUROPE
Charles the Great, or Charlemagne (742–814), united an empire covering much of modern France and Germany. He was a great Christian leader as well as a skilful warrior.

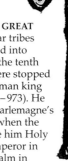

OTTO THE GREAT
The Magyar tribes that flooded into Europe in the tenth century were stopped by the German king Otto I (912–973). He became Charlemagne's successor when the Pope made him Holy Roman Emperor in 962. His realm in western Europe became known as the Holy Roman Empire.

THE DARK AGES
In the fifth century, the Roman Empire slowly fell apart as Germanic tribes from the north pushed across its frontiers, destroying towns and trade routes. Saxons settled in Britain, Franks took over Gaul (France), and Goths invaded Italy itself. In 476, the last Roman emperor lost his throne. These centuries of disorder became known as the "Dark" Ages, but this was not an entirely accurate description. Under the sixth-century emperor Justinian I, the Byzantine capital of Constantinople became one of the most magnificent cities in the world. By the eighth century, the great Frankish ruler Charlemagne had once more united a large part of Europe, encouraging the spread of learning and Christianity throughout his empire.

400–800

THE GREAT LEADERS
The Christian king Charlemagne supported the Pope as he tried to drive the barbarian invaders out of Italy, and in 800 the Pope crowned him "Holy Roman Emperor" in gratitude. Europe was threatened by invaders throughout the ninth and tenth centuries – Vikings raided the northern coasts, and the fierce Magyars pressed in from central Asia. But gradually new nations began to emerge. The lands of the Franks became France, Alfred the Great (871–899) defeated the Vikings to become king of England, and Otto I of Germany fought off the Magyars.

800–1000

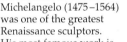

NORMANS NORTH AND SOUTH
As William of Normandy (c. 1027–1087) was conquering England in 1066, other Norman nobles were carving out an empire in Italy and Sicily.

THE CRUSADES
The Crusades (p. 28) began in 1095 as a Christian campaign to drive the Muslims out of the Holy Land. Jerusalem was captured in 1099, but later crusades were less successful.

German crusader's helmet

UNIFIER
This beautiful gilded head represents the powerful Holy Roman emperor Frederick I, or Barbarossa (1121–90), who brought unity to the German states in the 12th century.

THE GREAT PLAGUE
The Black Death had a lasting effect on European society. So many peasants died that there were hardly enough people left to farm the land. Increased demands on their labour caused the peasants to revolt in both France and England.

Bishop's crook, or crozier

THE CHURCH
The Catholic Church was one of the most powerful institutions of the Middle Ages. During the 13th century, the religious Inquisition was established to hunt out those who disagreed with its teachings. Those found guilty could be punished with excommunication (being cut off from the Church) or even death.

RENAISSANCE GENIUS
Michelangelo (1475–1564) was one of the greatest Renaissance sculptors. His most famous work is the beautiful marble statue, the *David*, now in Florence.

DISSOLVING THE MONASTERIES
When the English king Henry VIII (1491–1547) quarrelled with the Catholic Church, he appointed himself head of the Church in England and "dissolved" the great monasteries, taking their lands and property.

STABILITY
After 1000, life in Europe became more stable. Supported by the feudal system (p. 8), strong rulers brought order to the new nations. This encouraged trade and the growth of towns and cities, and the population rose. The Catholic Church (p. 30) reached the peak of its power as great cathedrals were built and new monastic orders were formed (p. 36). The first European university was founded in Italy.

PLAGUE AND WAR
The 14th century saw a series of disasters strike Europe. Bad harvests caused famine and the Black Death (p. 60) killed a third of the population. England and France began the Hundred Years' War in 1337, and church leaders squabbled over the title of pope. However, there was also an expansion in trade spearheaded in northern Europe by the prosperous Hanseatic League (p. 47).

NEW BEGINNINGS
The 15th century was a time of change. Scholars and artists explored new ideas and artistic styles in the Renaissance (p. 62), and in the 1500s religious reformers broke away from the Catholic Church in the Reformation (p. 62). This was also a great age of discovery. Explorers from Spain and Portugal crossed the Atlantic and Indian oceans, opening new horizons for trade and development (p. 63).

1000–1250

1250–1400

1400–1540

Medieval society

SOCIETY IN MUCH OF medieval Europe was organised into a "feudal" system, which was based on the allocation of land in return for services. The king gave grants of land, or fiefs, to his most important noblemen (barons and bishops) and in return, each noble promised to supply the king with soldiers in time of war. A noble pledged himself to be the king's servant, or vassal, at a special ceremony – kneeling before the king he swore an oath of loyalty with the words, "Sire, I become your man." The great nobles often divided their lands among lower lords, or knights, who in turn became their vassals. In this way, feudalism stretched from the top to the bottom of society. At the very bottom were the peasants who worked the land itself. They had few rights, little property – and no vassals.

TOP OF THE TREE
In this 14th-century picture, a French king presides over a gathering of his most important vassals, with the bishops on one side and barons on the other.

GOD'S DEPUTY
Medieval kings were seen as God's deputies on earth. A coronation was a magnificent religious ceremony when archbishops anointed the new king with holy oil as a sign of his status.

TAXES NOT AXES
By about 1100, many vassals were unwilling to fight for their king. Instead, they were allowed to pay a sum of cash, called "scutage", or shield money, which could be used to hire soldiers. Scutage was one of the first regular money taxes levied by kings from their noblemen. A system of tax-collectors (above) made sure that the full amounts were paid.

THE BARONS
Barons (p. 24) were the most powerful and wealthy noblemen, who received their fiefs directly from the king. When William of Normandy (p. 7) conquered England in 1066, he had about 120 barons. Each provided the king with a possible army of over 5,000 men.

THE LORDS
Lords ruled over fiefs or manors (p. 14), renting out most of their land to the peasants who worked for them. They were also the warriors of medieval society. As trained knights, they were bound by oath to serve the great nobles who granted them their fiefs, and could be called to battle at any time.

THE PEASANTS
The peasants were at the bottom of the feudal tree. They were the workers who farmed the land to provide food for everyone else. Most peasants worked for a lord who let them farm a piece of land for themselves in return for their labour (p. 10).

Bishop wears a mitre (p. 31) as a sign of his status

King is mockingly portrayed with a cat on his head!

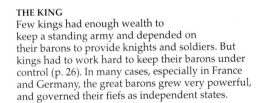

THE BISHOPS
Bishops could wield as much power as the barons. They ruled over areas called dioceses (p. 31), and all the priests and monasteries within them. The regular collection of tithes (p. 13) and other taxes from their dioceses made many bishops extremely rich.

THE KING
Few kings had enough wealth to keep a standing army and depended on their barons to provide knights and soldiers. But kings had to work hard to keep their barons under control (p. 26). In many cases, especially in France and Germany, the great barons grew very powerful, and governed their fiefs as independent states.

ROUGH JUSTICE
In the Middle Ages, ordinary people had few rights. Those who broke the law were tried in the court of their lord, who had almost complete power over them. Punishment for crimes was often harsh – a convicted criminal might be dragged behind a horse, whipped, locked in the stocks, or hanged, depending on the nature of his or her crime. But being at the top of the feudal system did not always ensure better treatment. Lords and barons sometimes had to pay their king large sums of money to get a fair trial. The medieval Church operated its own justice system with its own laws (the canon laws) and courts (p. 31) that were outside the jurisdiction of the king.

A peasant's life

Statue of a
French peasant
c. 1500

ACCORDING TO THE LAW, medieval peasants did not belong to themselves. Everything, including their land, their animals, their homes, their clothes, and even their food, belonged to the lord of the manor (p. 14). Known as serfs or villeins, peasants were bound to work for their lord, who allowed them to farm their own piece of land in return. Their lives were ones of almost constant toil. Most struggled to produce enough food to feed their families as well as fulfilling their duties to the lord. Forbidden from leaving the manor without permission, the only way for a peasant to gain freedom was by saving enough money to buy a plot of land, or by marrying a free person.

Simple spoons can be cut from horn

Shepherd's horn pipe

DAILY GRIND
Peasants worked hard every day except Sundays and holy days, in blazing sun, rain, or snow. Combined with a poor diet, it wasn't surprising that many European peasants in 1300 lived no longer than 25 years.

Tired peasant wipes the sweat from his brow

DO IT YOURSELF
Peasants made some of their own tools and utensils, although skilled craftsmen produced their pottery, leatherwork, and iron. Besides wood and leather, the most important material was horn from cattle or sheep. Light and strong, it did not absorb flavours like wood and did not require great energy to shape (p. 16). Horn spoons saved on washing-up, according to one writer, "with a little licking they will always be kept as clean as a die".

Wat Tyler is killed by a blow from a sword

THE PEASANTS' REVOLT
After the Black Death (pp. 60–61), there was a shortage of labour in 14th-century Europe. The peasants had to work harder than ever, and in England they also had to pay an extra tax. In 1381, the English peasants rose in rebellion. Led by Wat Tyler, they marched on London where they murdered the archbishop. When they met the king, Richard II (1367–1400), he agreed to end the new tax, but Wat Tyler was killed in a quarrel. The peasant mob swiftly disbanded and went home. The French Jacquerie revolt of 1358 ended much more bloodily when armoured knights slaughtered several thousand rebels.

Straw hat to protect the head on hot days

Cheap pewter badge for good luck

Felt hat decorated with a cockerel feather and a "fleur-de-lys" badge

Brown woollen jacket lined with linen

Blue woollen doublet fastened with laces, or points

Linen shirt

Linen underpants, or braes

Leather flask, or costrel, for carrying ale into the fields

Hose are tied to doublet with points

Peasants working with their hose rolled down

Woollen "split" hose can be rolled down for working

Leather working boots

PEASANT COTTAGE

Most peasants lived in simple homes like this reconstructed 13th-century cottage. The walls are made from local flint, but they were more often made from wattle and daub – woven strips of wood covered with a mixture of dung, straw, and clay. Inside, the floor was of bare, trampled earth. Most cottages had only one or two rooms which contained basic furniture such as a trestle table and bench, a chest for clothes, and straw mattresses to sleep on. There was a stone hearth in the centre of the main room, but no chimney, so it must have been very dark and smoky.

PLAIN CLOTHES

These are the kind of clothes that would have been worn by a peasant in the 1440s. Clothes, like tools, were mostly home-made from local materials. Peasant women spent much of their time spinning wool into coarse thread, which was then woven into cloth and made into garments. Sheepskin cloaks were worn in winter to keep out the cold and rain, and wooden pattens (p. 23) could be put on over leather boots in muddy conditions. Although outer clothes were never washed, linen underwear was laundered regularly. People's clothes generally smelled of woodsmoke which had a deodorizing effect!

Tied to the soil

IN MEDIEVAL EUROPE, more than 90 per cent of the population lived and worked on the land. Farming was a full-time job since methods were ancient and not very efficient. The crop-growing areas around a village were usually divided into three big fields. Peasants were allotted some land in each so that good and bad soil was shared out equally. They hoed and harvested their own plots, or strips, but worked together on big jobs such as ploughing and hay-making. A failed harvest could mean starvation for the whole village.

Wooden pitchfork for lifting hay and wheat-sheaves

HARVEST TIME
In late summer, women and children worked alongside the men to bring in the harvest. They cut the wheat with sickles, grasping each clump firmly so that the grains wouldn't shake loose. The wheat was then tied in bundles, or sheaves, set in stooks in the field to ripen, loaded onto a cart, and taken to the barn. Once the harvest was in, the wheat was threshed – beaten with a hinged stick, or flail, to loosen the grains from the ears.

SOWING THE SEED
In the "three-field system", only two fields were sown with crops in one year while the third was left empty, or fallow, so it could recover its strength. One field was sown with wheat in winter, and the next spring, the second was sown with rye, barley, or oats. Seeds were scattered, or broadcast, by hand.

Man knocking acorns out of an oak tree for his pigs

Seeds fell in the ploughed furrows, but many were lost to hungry birds

Farmer broadcasts the seeds in a sweeping arc

Basket of seeds called a seedlip

Shafts for pulling the cart

AUTUMN ACORNS
Every autumn, the lord of the manor allowed his serfs to run their pigs in his private woods, where they could feed on acorns and beechnuts. Sheep, geese, and goats grazed on common wasteland at the edge of the village. All the same, most animals were thin and wiry!

Hungry pig

Peasants working together at harvest time

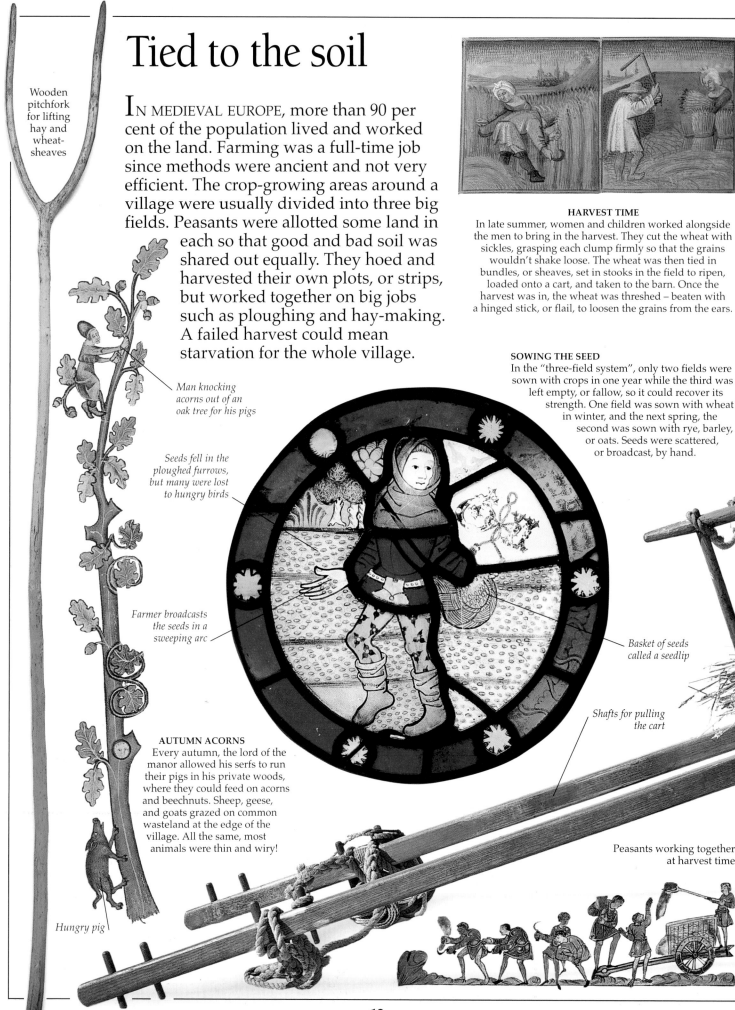

SHEAR PROFIT
Sheep shearing was the most important spring job in hilly regions of medieval Europe. Wool fetched high prices and its trade became one of the richest industries of the Middle Ages.

TITHE BARN
This huge 13th-century barn was used to store tithes. Villagers had to give the local priest a tenth, or tithe, of everything they produced, from crops and firewood, to eggs and flour. Tithes made some churches very wealthy – and very unpopular.

MANUAL LABOUR
With no machines, all farm work was done by hand using simple tools like these. Most jobs involved back-breaking labour, from breaking clods (lumps of soil) to hoeing young crops.

Billhook for maintaining hedges

Sickle for harvesting crops

Threshed wheat stalks, or straw

Rear gate is tied to keep the straw from falling out

Rim of wooden wheel is clad with six iron "strakes" for extra strength

CARTED OFF
Medieval peasants would have transported their wheat, straw, and hay in carts like this. Straw (the leftover stalks from the harvest) was used for numerous purposes, from thatching roofs to making mattresses. Hay was another important crop. Along with wheatstraw and dried beans, it provided the only winter feed for farm animals. Even then, there was rarely enough to go round and most cattle, pigs, and goats had to be killed in late autumn. Every peasant had a share in the village's hay meadow and hay-making was a communal task.

Large wheels allow the cart to ride over big bumps and ruts

Running a manor

MOST COUNTRY PEOPLE LIVED on a manor which consisted of a village, the lord's house or castle, a church, and the surrounding farmland. The lord of the manor governed the community and appointed officials who made sure that the villagers carried out their duties. These involved farming the lord's land, or demesne, and paying rents in the form of produce. The lord also acted as a judge in the manor court and had the power to fine those who broke the law. Since manors were often isolated, the villagers had to produce everything they needed themselves. Few goods, except salt for curing meat and iron for tools, came from outside. The only visitors were pedlars, pilgrims, or soldiers, and few people ever travelled far from their own village.

OTHER DUTIES
The lord was, first and foremost, a knight (p. 8) who provided men to fight for the king whenever he needed them. These knights are receiving their swords.

Steward discusses farm business with his lord

Medieval watering pot

THE STEWARD
The lord left the daily running of his manor to a number of officials. The most important was the steward, who organized farmwork, kept accounts of the estate's money, and presided at the manor court if his master was away. Stewards were well-paid, powerful figures in the district.

THE LORD AND LADY
The lord and lady of the manor had to oversee the running of the estate and their household, but they also had a fair amount of free time to pursue leisure activities. This French tapestry shows two angels holding a canopy over the heads of a noble and his lady, perhaps symbolizing their charmed lives!

THE MANOR HOUSE
The lord and his family lived in a large house that was often built of stone. It was surrounded by gardens and stables, and was protected by a high wall and sometimes by a moat. Apart from the church, the manor house was the centre of community life – its great hall served as the manor court and as the venue for special village feasts, such as those given after the harvest and at Christmas time.

Favourite hawks were carried everywhere, even into church!

Peak keeps the sun out of the eyes and, when reversed, allows rainwater to run off

Felt hat

Brown doublet

HAPPY HUNTING

...rds and ladies spent much of their ...ne hunting, which was considered a noble ...rsuit. Many kept hawks to fly after rabbits ...doves, and packs of hounds for chasing ...er or wild boar in their private woodland.

THE BAILIFF

Next in importance to the steward was the bailiff. He was usually a peasant, which can be seen from his clothes (right) – they were made from better cloth than those of a farm labourer, but were basically the same style. However, the bailiff was not a serf (p. 10), but a freeholder who owned his own land. He was in charge of allotting jobs to the peasants, looking after the demesne's cattle, and taking care of repairs to buildings and tools for which he hired skilled craftsmen such as carpenters and smiths.

Jacket has a longer cut than that of a labourer

GOING TO THE MILL

In most communities, there was only one watermill, which was owned by the lord. He banned all others, even handmills, so that the villagers were forced to carry their grain to his mill for grinding into flour. As payment, the lord kept some of their grain. Villagers might also have to bake their bread in the lord's oven and use his wine press for their grapes, for which they paid similar fees.

Woollen, linen-lined jacket with pewter buttons

THE REEVE

The reeve was the bailiff's right-hand man. He was a peasant, chosen by the other villagers. Carrying a white stick as a badge of office, the reeve supervised work on the lord's demesne, checking that everyone began on time, and ensuring that none of the produce was stolen.

Stirrups pulled the hose closer to the leg for a fashionably slender silhouette

Leather boots

A medieval home

MEDIEVAL HOMES WERE VERY DIFFERENT to ours. Peasants spent most of the daylight hours outside, so the draughts and little light from their unglazed windows did not trouble them. Inside, they kept below the smoke of the fire by sitting on low stools. For lighting, they peeled field rushes and dipped them in fat, which burned like small candles. Everything was kept as clean as possible – the earthen floors were often worn hollow as a result of constant sweeping. Domestic life was much more communal than ours, with whole families eating, sleeping, and spending free time together in their one- or two-roomed houses (p. 11).

The homes of the wealthy were much more elaborate. By the 13th century, some noblemen had a private family room, the solar. They paved their floors with decorated tiles and hung bright tapestries on their walls.

KEEPING WARM
Medieval homes had hearths in the centre of the room – away from wooden walls to avoid the risk of fire. By the 1400s, more people could afford stone chimneys, so fireplaces were more common.

WINDOW ON THE WORLD
It was possible to judge the social status of a household by looking at its windows. The poor had small holes covered with wooden shutters that could be closed at night or in cold weather. The better-off might have fenestral windows – lattice frames covered in linen that had been soaked in resin and tallow. These let in light and kept out draughts, and could be removed on fine days.

Shutters are closed at night

Unwound horn

Central part is split and polished

Curly sheep's horn

HORN OF PLENTY
Horn has been called the plastic of the Middle Ages because it was cheap and pliable. To make a horn window pane, the horn was first softened in water for three months, then unwound, split, and polished until it was transparent.

Urinal; urine was often saved to be used for cloth finishing and dyeing processes

Wattle-and-daub wall (p. 11)

Some castle privies emptied directly into the moat!

THE SMALLEST ROOM
By the late 15th century, many houses had an indoor privy. It was little more than a closet in the wall with a hole over a cess-pit. There probably would have been an outdoor privy as well.

Horn panes are slotted into a wooden window frame

GLASS SUBSTITUTE
In the Middle Ages, glass was rare and expensive and only churches or royal palaces could afford glass windows. Noblemen and merchants often made do with windows made from panes of polished horn. These were cheaper and tougher than glass and let in lots of light, although they were a bit difficult to see through.

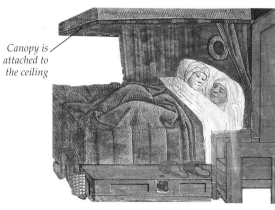

ROCK-A-BYE BABY
This noble baby's rocking cradle was probably the most comfortable bed in the house. However, babyhood was a dangerous time – more than one in three infants died, usually from disease.

Cradle can be rocked by mother's foot while she sews or spins

SEATS TO SUIT
In most homes, people sat on plain stools or benches. Only a lord was likely to have a chair with a back and armrests, and he was thus called the "chairman".

Canopy is attached to the ceiling

BED-TIME
A 15th-century servants' book gives strict instructions on putting the lord to bed. After undressing him, combing his hair and pulling on his nightcap, the servant should, "draw the curtains round about the bed, set there his night-light, drive out the dog and cat, giving them a clout, take no leave of your lord, but bow low to him and retire".

White rose of the Virgin Mary; many decorations bore religious motifs

Canopy, or tester

HANGINGS
Painted linen, woven tapestries, and fine wool cloths were hung from walls and doorways. They made rooms warmer by keeping out draughts and providing insulation. They also added brightness to dim interiors. This doorway and painted linen wall-hanging come from the home of a wealthy merchant.

Warm, woollen curtains keep out draughts

Linen pillow stuffed with chopped straw

Linen sheet

Woven straw mattress

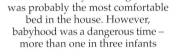

Lavender Tansy Ladies' bedstraw

KEEPING BUGS AT BAY
Herbs such as lavender, tansy, and ladies' bedstraw were strewn on straw mattresses. Their strong scents not only made the bed smell sweeter, but also kept away fleas.

Woollen blanket

"Truckle" bed can be wheeled out for children, servants, and others to sleep on

A ROOM WITHIN A ROOM
Better-off people slept in beds made from strong timber beams with a canopy overhead and curtains at the sides. The rich may have had feather-filled mattresses, but most people's were made of straw. When the curtains were drawn, the bed became a snug, private space. This bed would have belonged to a bailiff (p. 15) in the late 15th or early 16th century.

From kitchen to table

People's diets in the Middle Ages varied according to their means. Rich noblemen and merchants could afford to eat a wide range of food (p. 20) including expensive dried fruits, almonds, and spices from Asia. Although one poet believed the poor should live on "nettles, reeds, briars, and peashells", their diet was generally better than that. Ordinary people ate dark, coarse bread made from wheat mixed with rye or oatmeal, garden vegetables, and meat, especially pork, from their livestock. During the winter, they had to make do with meat and fish that had been preserved in salt, and cooks devised clever ways of masking the taste by adding oatmeal, peas, beans, or breadcrumbs to the pot. Cows, sheep, and goats provided milk for dairy foods which were known as "white meats".

Small pot-hanger

Adjustable ratchet

Large pot-hook for a huge cauldron

HOOKS FOR COOKS

Most people boiled their food in iron pots that either hung from hooks over the fire or stood in the hot ashes. Once cooked, chunks of meat were pulled out of the pot with a flesh-hook. Vegetables and grains were added to the leftover liquid to make a soupy "pottage" which was a staple part of everyone's diet. This could be turned into thick pudding called frumenty by mixing it with wheat, crushed almonds, and egg yolks.

Flesh-hook for removing meat from a boiling cauldron

Fresh river trout

FAST FOOD

The Church ordered that Wednesdays, Fridays, and Saturdays were "fast" days, when no meat should be eaten. Fish was allowed and became a vital part of the diet. Ordinary people ate mainly salted or pickled herring, fresh eels, and shellfish. The wealthy could eat carp and pike from their fishponds and a wide variety of river and sea fish.

Pot-hook is suspended from an adjustable pot-hanger to allow the cauldron to be raised or lowered into the fire

Pot stand, or trivet

Stone hearth

Firewood

Three-legged cauldron can stand in the fire or hang from a pot-hook

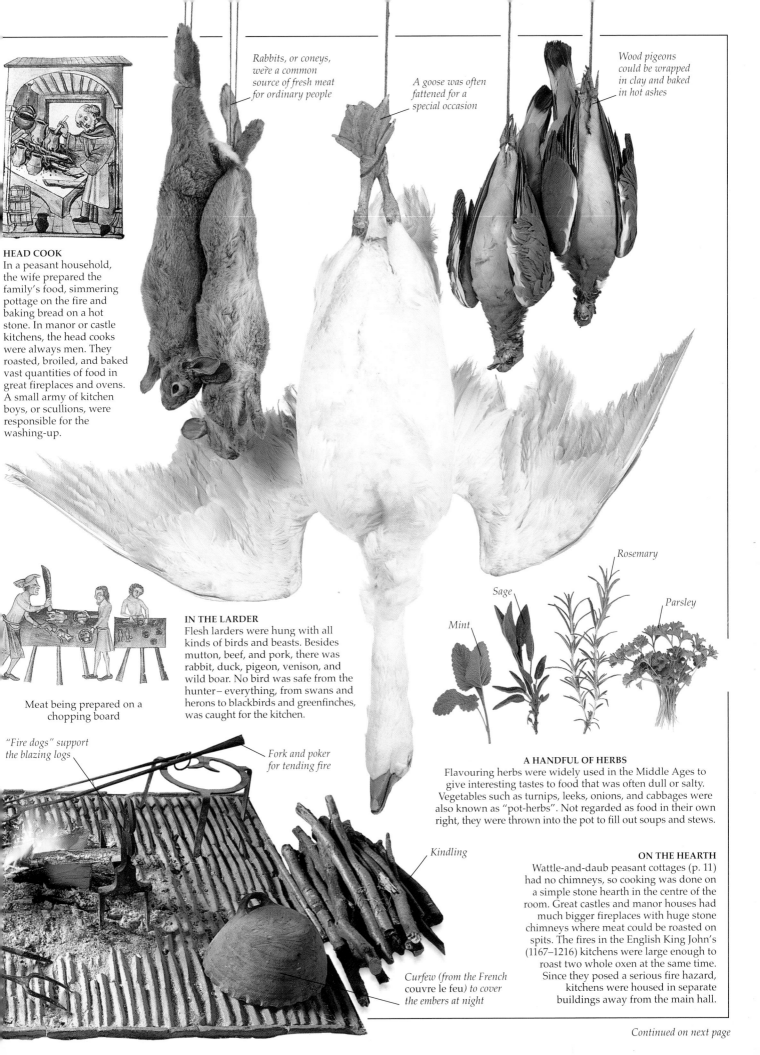

HEAD COOK
In a peasant household, the wife prepared the family's food, simmering pottage on the fire and baking bread on a hot stone. In manor or castle kitchens, the head cooks were always men. They roasted, broiled, and baked vast quantities of food in great fireplaces and ovens. A small army of kitchen boys, or scullions, were responsible for the washing-up.

Rabbits, or coneys, were a common source of fresh meat for ordinary people

A goose was often fattened for a special occasion

Wood pigeons could be wrapped in clay and baked in hot ashes

Meat being prepared on a chopping board

IN THE LARDER
Flesh larders were hung with all kinds of birds and beasts. Besides mutton, beef, and pork, there was rabbit, duck, pigeon, venison, and wild boar. No bird was safe from the hunter – everything, from swans and herons to blackbirds and greenfinches, was caught for the kitchen.

Rosemary

Sage

Mint

Parsley

"Fire dogs" support the blazing logs

Fork and poker for tending fire

A HANDFUL OF HERBS
Flavouring herbs were widely used in the Middle Ages to give interesting tastes to food that was often dull or salty. Vegetables such as turnips, leeks, onions, and cabbages were also known as "pot-herbs". Not regarded as food in their own right, they were thrown into the pot to fill out soups and stews.

Kindling

ON THE HEARTH
Wattle-and-daub peasant cottages (p. 11) had no chimneys, so cooking was done on a simple stone hearth in the centre of the room. Great castles and manor houses had much bigger fireplaces with huge stone chimneys where meat could be roasted on spits. The fires in the English King John's (1167–1216) kitchens were large enough to roast two whole oxen at the same time. Since they posed a serious fire hazard, kitchens were housed in separate buildings away from the main hall.

Curfew (from the French couvre le feu) *to cover the embers at night*

Continued on next page

High table, low table

Dinner was the grandest and biggest meal of the day. The lord of the manor sat with his most important guests at the "high" table, raised on a platform, or dais, at one end of the great hall. From here, he could look down on the lesser diners and members of his household sitting at the "low" tables. A feast might have three courses of cooked meats and fish, elaborate roasts of swans and peacocks re-clothed in their skins, followed by numerous sweet and spicy dishes. All of these were quickly carried from the nearby kitchen so that they arrived piping hot. The lord was served first, after a sample of the food had been tasted by a servant to make sure it was not poisoned. Only then were the other diners served.

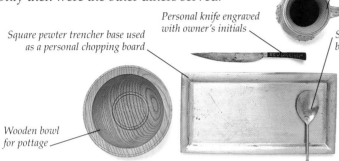

Drinking vessel

Square pewter trencher base used as a personal chopping board

Personal knife engraved with owner's initials

Spoon was provided by the house

Wooden bowl for pottage

GET SET
In the Middle Ages, table forks did not exist, but everyone used their own knife, a spoon, strips of bread, and their fingers to eat very politely, for table manners were important and formed part of every wealthy child's education.

ENTERTAINING IN STYLE
At the high table, the lord sat on a bench at the centre with his back to the wall. Guests were seated next to him in order of importance, starting with churchmen, then noblemen, then the lord's family. Servants scurried to and fro with meats, sauces, and jugs of wine from the buttery (bottlery). Singers and acrobats often entertained the diners between courses.

The lord's seat at the centre of the table

High table stood on a raised platform called a dais

Expensive tiled floor

Large jug for ale

Large wooden
platter for serving
bread or meat

Horn mug

Leather
tankard

Trestle table

Spoons were placed face
down to "keep out the devil"

Hard wooden bench

BANQUET BUSTLE

The banqueting hall could be a crowded, noisy, smelly place. Tables were crammed with diners and dogs crunched bones on the floor. Only the lord got a serving to himself. Other diners shared a bowl with up to three fellow guests. Most ate with their fingers, so it was important that these were clean and not used for blowing noses or scratching. Table etiquette was strict: "If it happen that you cannot help scratching," one writer advised, "then courteously take a portion of your dress, and scratch with that."

COMMON FARE

Diners seated at a low table would have eaten less elaborate food than that served up for the lord, but there were some common foods. Pottage, a thick broth of vegetables and meat stock, was a staple, everyday dish often served as a first course at feasts. Apart from pottage, everyone ate bread. All food was served on thick slices of stale bread called trenchers and small loaves called manchets were used for mopping up gravy.

Expensive
wine glass

Wooden
drinking bowl

Glazed ceramic
drinking vessel

Decorated ceramic
jug for wine or ale

"Double-salt" for
salt and mustard

Dyed cloth
wall-cover

Linen tablecloth was
"ironed" while damp using
round glass linen smoothers

LAID FOR A LORD

The high table was carefully set out with a clean linen tablecloth, trencher bases, pottage and drinking bowls, salt, jugs, and, if the household was wealthy, fine glasses. In the 15th century, a large communal napkin called the long towel was spread over the knees of the diners once they were seated.

Medieval women

"I⊤ IS CLEAR", wrote a French priest in 1386, "that man is much nobler than woman, and of greater virtue". The medieval Church looked on women as inferior to men, and taught that they should be meek, and obedient to their fathers and husbands. But the real lives of women in the Middle Ages were rather different. Not all of them stayed quietly at home, because most had to work for a living. Peasant women toiled alongside their husbands in the fields as well as having to feed and clothe their families. The wives and daughters of craftsmen were often employed in the workshop and frequently operated as tradeswomen in their own right, and wealthy ladies organized large households and sometimes ran their husbands' affairs. However, only a few powerful abbesses, noblewomen, and queens had any influence on national events.

KEEP IT COVERED
Although young single women often wore their hair loose, married women were expected to keep their hair covered in a linen "wimple" as a sign of modesty.

THE MAID OF ORLEANS
St Joan (1412–1431) was a French peasant's daughter who, at the age of 13, heard voices telling her to drive the invading English army out of France. Dressed in armour, she led the French troops to a great victory at the besieged town of Orleans. However, Joan was later betrayed and sold to the English, who burned her as a witch.

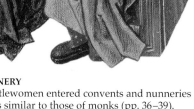

GET THEE TO A NUNNERY
Many unmarried gentlewomen entered convents and nunneries where they lived lives similar to those of monks (pp. 36–39). Nunneries offered women the opportunity to lead a devout life and also to obtain an education and take on responsibilities denied them in the outside world. As local landowners and employers, many abbesses were important figures in the community (above).

WOMEN OF WEALTH
Landowners, male or female, were powerful figures in medieval society, and an unmarried woman of property had equal legal rights with men. She could make a will, and sign documents with her own seal – this 13th-century seal belonged to a French noblewoman called Elizabeth of Sevorc. However, when a woman married, she forfeited her land and rights to her husband. On his death she was entitled to a third of his land with which to support herself.

HOLDING THE FORT
This noblewoman has collapsed on hearing of her husband's death. Many women took on the responsibility of running large estates when their husbands died in battle or were away at court or on a crusade (p. 28). They settled local disputes, managed the farms, and handled finances. Some women even fought battles, defending their castles when they were under siege.

SPINSTERS

Spinning was done almost entirely by women using hand-held spindles like this one (the spinning wheel was introduced from India in the 13th century). Many single women earned a living in this way, hence the term "spinster" for an unmarried woman.

Wool twists into thread as the spindle twirls

WRAP UP

Most women covered their hair with white linen head-wraps, but the wealthy wore gold nets over their coiled plaits. The well-known pointed hat called the hennin was only popular for a short time in the late 15th century.

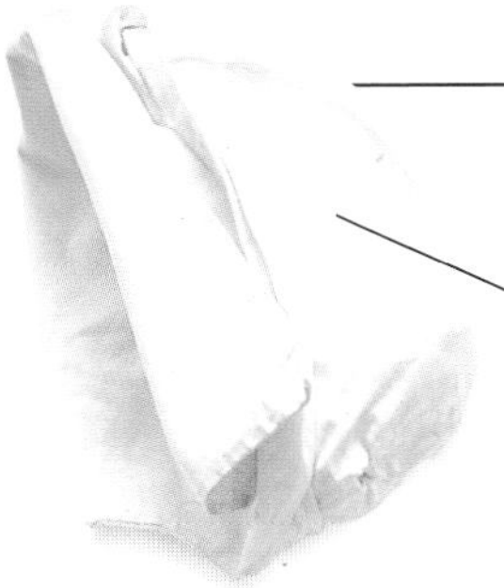

Linen head-wrap keeps hair clean as well as hidden

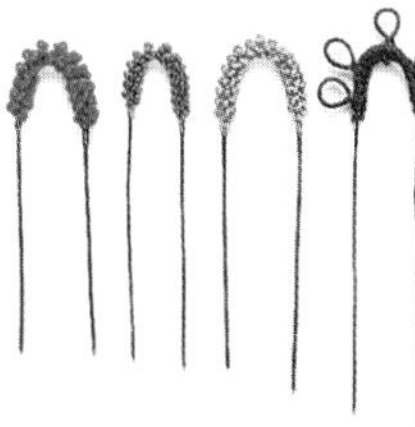

Decorated hair pins

Linen shift

Prayer beads

Pin-on sleeves worn on Sundays and special occasions

AN EARLY FEMINIST

Christine de Pisan (1364–1429) was one of the few medieval women to earn a living by writing. She wrote poetry and books protesting at the way women were both glorified and insulted by male authors.

THE TOWNSWOMAN

A middle-class townswoman might have worn these clothes in the 15th century. In the towns, women worked in a variety of occupations. They might be shopkeepers, spinners, bakers, or "alewives" who brewed ale. Both married and unmarried women worked for a living, often combining two or more jobs because they were paid less than men.

Woollen "kirtle" fits close around the upper body

Leather purse serves as a pocket

Leather garters to hold up stockings

Buckled leather shoes with thin soles

Woollen, over-the-knee stockings

Wooden "pattens" worn over shoes when muddy

The great barons

EVERY NOBLEMAN was a vassal (p. 8) who had promised to serve his king. But many nobles grew so powerful that kings could not control them. By the 12th century, the strongest barons ruled what were really tiny, self-contained states with their own laws. The finery of their castle-courts often rivalled that of the king's, and many kept permanent armies at their beck and call. One French baron, the Sire de Coucy, had a bodyguard of 50 knights, each with ten followers. These small private armies sometimes rode out to plunder their neighbours in savage and pitiless raids, and they posed a serious threat to the king if he did not keep his barons happy.

PARLIAMENTARY PIONEER
The English king usually governed through a Great Council of barons and churchmen. But Simon de Montfort (c. 1208–65) wanted to limit the powers of Henry III (1207–72). He led a rebellion in 1264, took the king prisoner and summoned the first "parliament". This was made up of the old Council, plus two representatives from each shire and town.

HIT MEN
Barons sometimes hired mercenary troops to do their fighting for them. These were bands of up to 3,000 soldiers of all nationalities – deserters from the Crusades, outlaws, and exiled knights.

Composite 15th-century flag

VLAD DRACUL
Most infamous of all barons was the ghoulish Vlad Tepes of Romania (c. 1430–1476). According to legend, he put thousands of people to death by impaling them on stakes. He was nicknamed "Dracula", or "Dragon's son".

RALLY ROUND THE FLAG
Every nobleman had a banner such as this showing his own colours and emblems. Such flags were important rallying points for soldiers and knights on the battlefield.

THE BOAST OF HERALDRY
When knights rode into battle, their faces were hidden behind armour, so they identified themselves by carrying a coat of arms, or device, on their shield. By the 13th century, these devices were used not just by warriors, but by powerful baronial families.

WARLORD
Charging full-tilt at a band of helpless civilians, a fully armoured knight, with his face hidden behind a great helmet, was a chilling sight. Describing an attack by the men of a great baron on the town of Durham, England, in 1143, a monk recounted: "All that came in their way was destroyed; men were hung from the walls of their own houses; others they plunged into the bed of the river; everywhere throughout the town there were groans and all kinds of deaths."

14th-century visored "basinet"

THE GREAT CHARTER
In June 1215, the English barons forced King John (1167–1216) to sign the Magna Carta (Great Charter). This document limited the king's rights to tax the barons and to punish any man without a proper trial. But the Magna Carta did not recommend equal rights for all – ordinary people were scarcely mentioned. However, it was a crucial moment, the first time an English king had come under the control of the law.

King John's Great Seal

Wheel pommel

Italian war hammer, late 15th century

German battle axe, late 15th century

Single-handed French sword, 14th century

Fortified gatehouse

MORTAL COMBAT
The baron sat as judge in his own law court. If he could not reach a clear decision, he might allow a trial by combat. Accused and accuser would put on armour and fight each other with sword and axe – whoever won the battle, won the case. Most people preferred to hire champions to fight for them. But this was not a popular line of work. The loser might be suspected of surrendering on purpose, and have his hand chopped off as a punishment!

Double-edged blade with numerous battle-scars

FORTIFIED TOWNS
To protect themselves in times of war, medieval people built fortifications. The strong stone walls of castles could be seen all over the countryside, and most towns were also protected with walls, towers, and gatehouses. Some of these fortifications were massive, and the walls could be as much as 10 m (33 ft) thick. The town of Carcassone in France (above) still has 54 towers and medieval walls, that enclose the whole town.

The royal court

THE ROYAL COURT was the centre and the showpiece of the kingdom. Here a monarch demonstrated his power with grand ceremonies and banquets, collected taxes, settled disputes, and made laws. It was particularly important to maintain control over the powerful barons. Henry II of England (1133–1189) held special court sessions to sort out arguments over land-holding, and Louis IX of France (1214–1270) insisted on listening to cases in person. Other monarchs amazed their subjects and visitors alike with the magnificence of their courts. Most astounding of all were the Sicilian castles of the Holy Roman Emperor (p. 8) Frederick II (1194–1250), which had golden floors, exotic animals, beautiful gardens, and dancing girls.

Love-heart decorated with tears

THE RIGHT TO RULE
Most medieval kings believed they had absolute power over their subjects, given to them by God. This sometimes led them to arrogant gestures – and disaster. Richard II of England (1367–1400) once sat for hours on his throne, glancing around. He merely wanted to watch his courtiers kneel when he looked at them. By 1399, Richard's despotic ways had made him so unpopular that he was deposed from his throne.

Lances measure about 4 m (13 ft)

LYRICS OF LOVE
Every court had its minstrels, who sang songs about love and brave deeds, accompanying themselves on the harp or the lute (p. 44). The greatest love songs were written by the troubadours, who flourished in southern France in the 12th century. Each troubadour wrote in praise of his idealized lady love.

LANCE A LOT
To rebel against the king was equivalent to defying God, but if a king was weak or poor, his powerful barons could be troublesome (pp. 24–25). Monarchs were eager to lure their noblemen to court, where they could keep an eye on them. One great attraction was the joust, a contest of fighting skills. Here, two armoured knights cantered towards each other, their lances held before them. The object was to hit your opponent on the head or chest and knock him off his horse.

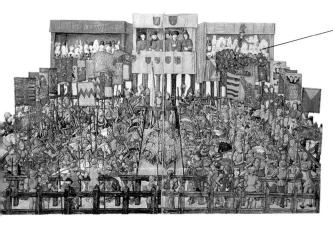

Court ladies watch the tournament from the stand

Glittering shield may have been presented as a tournament prize

WAR GAMES

Pomp and ceremony were important parts of court life. The mock battle, or tourney, was a popular and spectacular way of amusing the court in the 11th century. While the king, queen, and courtiers looked on, large parties of knights charged at each other. If they were unhorsed, they went on fighting on foot. Tourneys were bloody and dangerous – during one fight at Cologne, more than 60 knights were killed.

"Tables" counter for playing a game similar to backgammon

IDLE PASTIMES

The lords and ladies of the court whiled away idle hours with indoor games such as backgammon, chess, and dice. Playing cards became popular in the 13th century.

OFFICIAL BUSINESS

The king made his wishes known through writs. His scribe's office produced hundreds of documents each year granting lands, and permission to raise armies, appoint officials, and order the payment of taxes. This writ, dated 1291, is a grant of game rights from Edward I of England (1239–1307) to one of his barons, Roger de Pilkington.

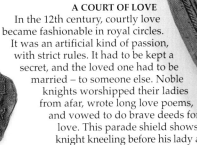

The royal seal makes the document official

A COURT OF LOVE

In the 12th century, courtly love became fashionable in royal circles. It was an artificial kind of passion, with strict rules. It had to be kept a secret, and the loved one had to be married – to someone else. Noble knights worshipped their ladies from afar, wrote long love poems, and vowed to do brave deeds for love. This parade shield shows a knight kneeling before his lady and bears the motto, "You, or Death".

15th-century Flemish shield

The medieval soldier

Peace was rare in medieval times especially in Europe. The Crusades against the Muslim Turks lasted for three centuries and the Hundred Years' War between England and France dragged on from 1337 to 1453. Even when there were no major campaigns, barons and brigands raided their neighbours. In the early Middle Ages, the armoured knight ruled the battlefield. He scorned the footsoldiers, who were mostly a rabble of poor, terrified, and untrained peasants pressed into battle by their lords. But by the 15th century, knights were fast going out of fashion and the common soldier became much more important. He developed into a professional warrior, well-paid, skilful with his weapon, and used to obeying orders. Many even worked as mercenary soldiers, hiring themselves out to the highest bidder.

THE CRUSADES
In 1095, the Pope called for a holy war against the Muslim Turks who controlled the Christian Holy Land of Palestine. A European army set of on the First Crusade and managed t recapture the holy city of Jerusalem but the Turks soon advanced again In all, there were eight crusades between 1147 and 1270, all of them failures. This 15th-century painting shows crusaders arriving at Damietta in Egypt.

ARCH ENEMY
Archers played a key role in the decline of the knight in the 15th century. Fired at the enemy from a safe distance, a deadly hail of arrows killed men and horses alike. Without their horses, heavily armoured knights were easy prey for footsoldiers.

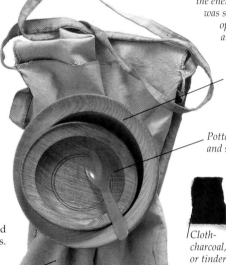

"Glaive", a form of pole-weapon used for stabbing or knocking the enemy aside; it was safer to keep opponents at arm's length

Wooden drinking bowl for ale

Pottage bowl and spoon

Canvas kit bag

Cloth-charcoal, or tinder

Steel

Flint

Flint, steel, and tinder for lighting camp fires

Chain splints keep swords from slicing through the arm

Leather boots generally lasted about three months

FOOTSORE AND HUNGRY
Life on the march could be very hard. A footsoldier would have to walk at least 10 km (6 miles) a day, and occasionally three times as far. His food bowl was often empty, for a large army soon consumed everything edible in the surrounding countryside. Starving French soldiers in the First Crusade of 1097 were told to feed on their enemies: "Are there not corpses of Turks in plenty? Cooked and salted they will be good to eat"!

Sheepskin mitten worn inside

Mitten gauntlet protects the hand and wrist

Peak protects the neck

Military "bollock" dagger

Eating knife

Visor limits vision, so was only lowered in fierce fighting

"Sallet" helmet

HANDSOME RANSOM
A captured enemy could be a valuable acquisition. Important prisoners were often held to ransom for large sums of money. When King Richard I of England (1157–99) was captured in 1194, his country had to pay 150,000 marks – a huge sum in those days.

BELT-BAG
A soldier had to carry his personal belongings with him wherever he went, so luggage was kept to a minimum. Slung from his belt, this leather purse probably contained money, dice for gambling, needles and thread, and a kerchief.

HAND-TO-HAND FIGHTING
With a sword in his right hand and a buckler in his left, a soldier was a dangerous enemy. The buckler was not only used to deflect blows, but also to hit an opponent in the face, before jabbing or slashing with the sword. However, the soldier did most of his fighting with a pole-weapon, and relied on his sword as a last resort. There were no rules of combat in medieval warfare, and most battles were terrifying free-for-alls.

Gauntlet limits wrist movement

Small fist-shield, or buckler, for punching

I'M ALRIGHT JACK
This military outfit would have been worn by a professional footsoldier in the late 15th century. Some of his kit would have been issued to him, and the rest was probably stolen, or looted. Most soldiers at this time wore much less armour than the knights of old. A padded tunic called a jack, with iron gauntlets and arm splints, gave good protection against sword and dagger cuts.

Thin leather belt

Close-fitting canvas "arming" doublet

Quilted "jack" made from multi-layered canvas

Single-handed sword for hand-to-hand combat

The Church

THE CATHOLIC CHURCH was at the centre of the medieval world. Unlike today, it was the only Church in Europe, and all Christians belonged to it. With its own laws, lands, and taxes, the Church was a powerful institution. It governed almost every aspect of people's lives, from the practical to the spiritual. Most men and women, rich and poor, were baptized and married in church, and attended mass every Sunday of their lives. When they died, their priest read them the last rites, and they were buried on church ground. For many, life on earth was hard and short, but the Church stated that if they followed the teachings of Christ, they would at least be rewarded in heaven. This idea gave the Church great power over people's hearts and minds.

LEADERS OF MEN
Archbishops were powerful men who sat on the king's council and played a leading role in government.

BIRD OF BLESSING
Suspended above the altar, this golden dove symbolized the Holy Spirit during the Eucharist – the Catholic ceremony where bread and wine are blessed and eaten to commemorate the sacrifice of Christ.

Censer is suspended on gilded chains

CHURCH TREASURES
By the 14th century, the Church had grown hugely wealthy. Money poured in from rents, tithes (p. 13), and the sale of indulgences (pardons for sins). Larger churches could afford to buy expensive sacramental vessels like this beautiful 14th-century silver chalice.

PARISH PRACTICES
The life of a parish priest was often a hard one. Many were poor men who lacked any serious education. Most of a priest's income came from fees charged for baptisms (above), marriages, and burial services. He also had his own land in the village, called the glebe, where he grew his own food. Apart from preaching, a village priest tended to the sick and poor, and the better-educated taught Latin and bible stories to local boys.

Burning incense is placed inside the censer

SWINGING CENSERS
During mass, priests swung censers full of burning incense. People believed that if they attended mass regularly, they would be rewarded by God – and the more masses, the greater the reward. The wealthy could pay to have the "Trental", or 30 masses, said for them.

CONDEMNED TO THE FLAMES

Few people challenged the authority of the Church, but those who did were severely punished. People who disagreed with the Church's teachings were called heretics. They faced being brought to trial in a church court and, under its special laws, could be condemned to be whipped or burned at the stake. The Cathar sect of southern France rejected the beliefs of the Catholic Church with their claims that everything on earth was created by the devil. In 1208, the Pope ordered a crusade against them. Over the next 26 years, thousands of Cathars were tortured and burned in huge bonfires until they had been completely wiped out.

VISIONS OF HELL

The Church taught that when a person died, the good and bad deeds of their life were literally weighed in the balance by God. Their soul was either carried to heaven by angels or dragged off to hell by demons. Hell was a real and terrifying place for people in medieval times, and its torments were pictured in vivid detail by numerous painters.

Angel swings a golden censer

Carved wooden angels from a medieval church nave (p. 39)

Angel holds a tiny church

Picture shows the coronation of the Virgin by Christ

Angel holds a gilded casket

BISHOP'S MITRE

Bishops were the local leaders of the Church. From their great cathedrals, they ruled over groups of parishes called dioceses. They usually came from noble families and were involved in affairs of state as well as those of the Church. Some were pious and learned men, but others were not – one 13th-century Italian bishop admitted that he did not believe in Christianity, and had only taken the office "because of its riches and honours".

14th-century bishop's hat, or mitre

VICAR OF CHRIST

The Pope was head of the whole Church and represented God on earth. This massive gilt ring belonged to Pope Eugenius IV, who ruled from 1431 to 1437.

Building a cathedral

In the early Middle Ages, large churches were built in the Roman style. They had massive pillars and thick walls to hold up the round-arched roofs. As a result, windows were small, and Romanesque churches were sometimes dark and gloomy. By the 12th century, they were too small for the booming population of Europe, and for the growing stream of pilgrims (pp. 42–43). There was an explosion of cathedral building, starting in 1140 with the Abbey of St Denis near Paris. This was constructed in a startling new style, called Gothic, where the weight of the roof rested not on the walls, but on outside supports called buttresses. This allowed walls to be thinner, and pierced with tall windows that led the eye heavenwards and flooded the cathedral with light.

SYMPHONIES IN STONE
Before 1350, 80 cathedrals were built in France alone. Among the first to use flying buttresses was Reims Cathedral, begun in 1211.

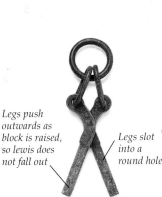

Tapered slot stops the legs sliding out

Shackle

The middle leg fits in last, wedging the other two firmly in place

LIFTING WITH A LEWIS
Medieval stonemasons (pp. 52-53) used lifting devices called lewises to raise heavy stone blocks. The legs fitted into a tapered slot cut into the top of the stone (shown in cross-section above), and the lifting rope was hooked onto the shackle at the top. This small (modern) lewis can lift blocks weighing up to a tonne.

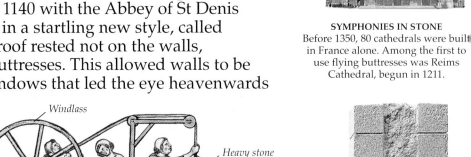

Windlass

Heavy stone blocks raised in a basket

Mortar carrier

Mason preparing blocks

MEN AT WORK
As the walls rose, masons had to work at greater heights. They stood on precarious wooden scaffolding lashed together with ropes. The stone was lifted up to them by a hoist, or windlass, attached to a big wheel turned by a man walking inside it. Working conditions were hazardous and there were many deaths.

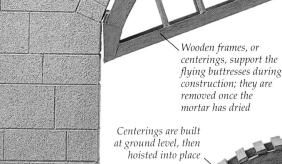

Wooden frames, or centerings, support the flying buttresses during construction; they are removed once the mortar has dried

Centerings are built at ground level, then hoisted into place

Legs push outwards as block is raised, so lewis does not fall out

Legs slot into a round hole

TIMELESS TOOLS
Lewises, like most other masonry tools (pp. 52–53), have changed little since medieval times. This kind of two-legged lewis was commonly used in the Middle Ages.

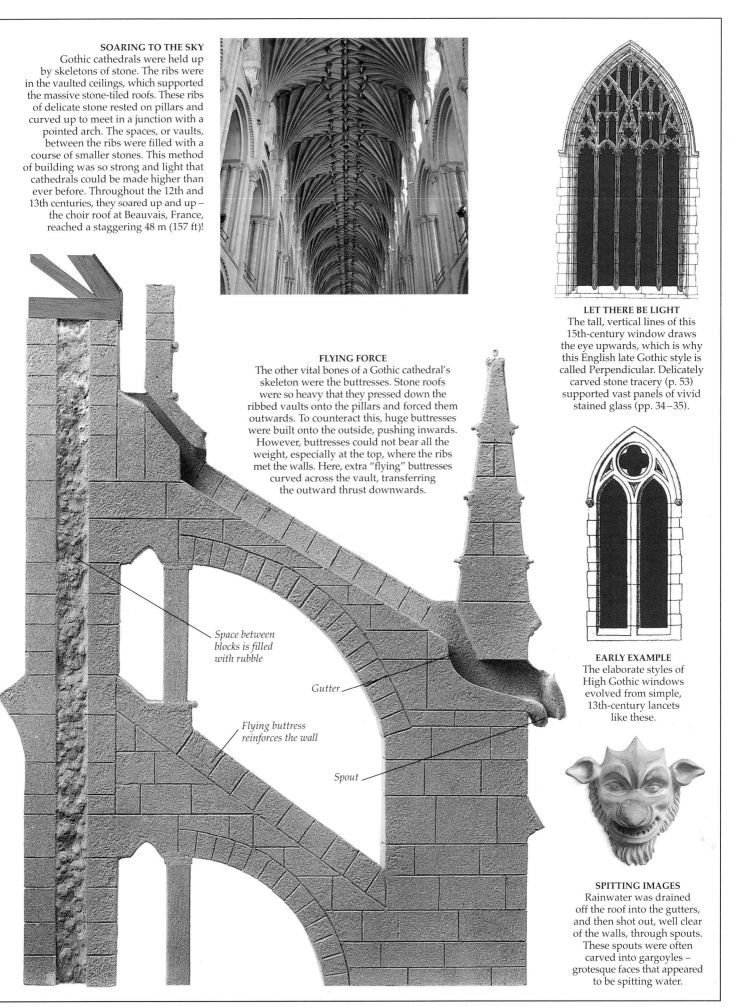

SOARING TO THE SKY
Gothic cathedrals were held up by skeletons of stone. The ribs were in the vaulted ceilings, which supported the massive stone-tiled roofs. These ribs of delicate stone rested on pillars and curved up to meet in a junction with a pointed arch. The spaces, or vaults, between the ribs were filled with a course of smaller stones. This method of building was so strong and light that cathedrals could be made higher than ever before. Throughout the 12th and 13th centuries, they soared up and up – the choir roof at Beauvais, France, reached a staggering 48 m (157 ft)!

FLYING FORCE
The other vital bones of a Gothic cathedral's skeleton were the buttresses. Stone roofs were so heavy that they pressed down the ribbed vaults onto the pillars and forced them outwards. To counteract this, huge buttresses were built onto the outside, pushing inwards. However, buttresses could not bear all the weight, especially at the top, where the ribs met the walls. Here, extra "flying" buttresses curved across the vault, transferring the outward thrust downwards.

Space between blocks is filled with rubble

Gutter

Flying buttress reinforces the wall

Spout

LET THERE BE LIGHT
The tall, vertical lines of this 15th-century window draws the eye upwards, which is why this English late Gothic style is called Perpendicular. Delicately carved stone tracery (p. 53) supported vast panels of vivid stained glass (pp. 34–35).

EARLY EXAMPLE
The elaborate styles of High Gothic windows evolved from simple, 13th-century lancets like these.

SPITTING IMAGES
Rainwater was drained off the roof into the gutters, and then shot out, well clear of the walls, through spouts. These spouts were often carved into gargoyles – grotesque faces that appeared to be spitting water.

33

The art of decoration

"I AM A POOR OLD WOMAN who knows nothing, who cannot read. But in the Church I see Paradise painted, and Hell where the damned broil." These were the words of a 15th-century French woman, and they spoke for millions of uneducated people in medieval Europe. For them, cathedrals and churches were not just places of worship, they were picture books and art galleries. The great cathedrals were filled with statues and carvings, painted panels and frescoes, which told stories of saints and biblical characters. Most wonderful of all were the stained glass windows through which light streamed in dazzling, brilliant colours.

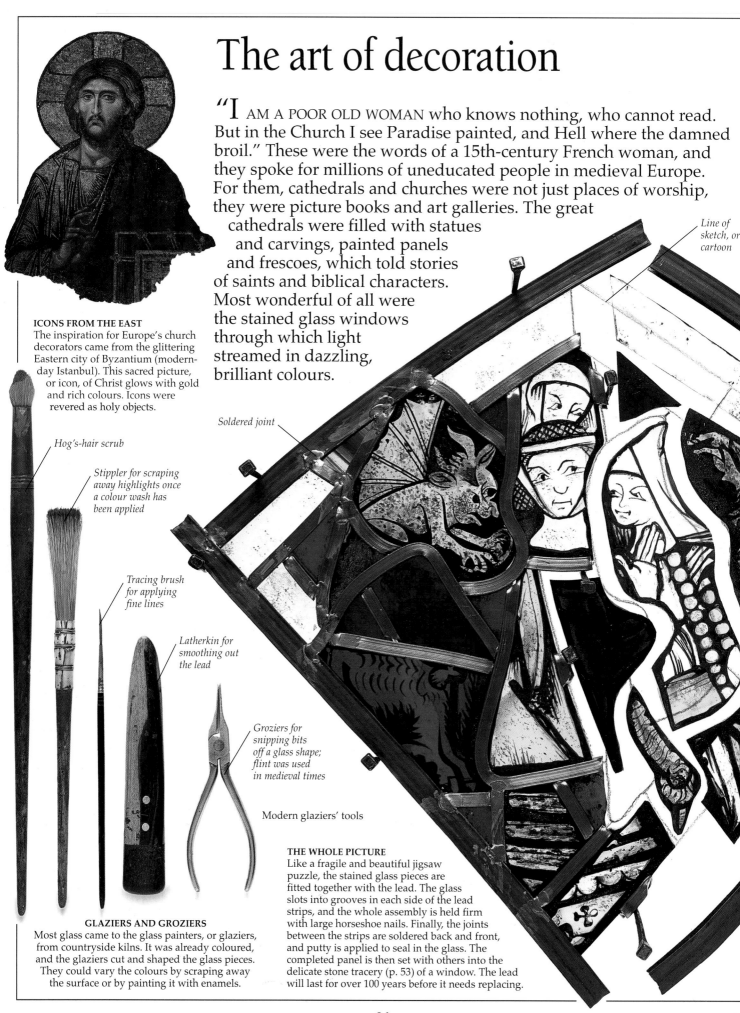

ICONS FROM THE EAST
The inspiration for Europe's church decorators came from the glittering Eastern city of Byzantium (modern-day Istanbul). This sacred picture, or icon, of Christ glows with gold and rich colours. Icons were revered as holy objects.

Hog's-hair scrub

Stippler for scraping away highlights once a colour wash has been applied

Tracing brush for applying fine lines

Latherkin for smoothing out the lead

Groziers for snipping bits off a glass shape; flint was used in medieval times

Modern glaziers' tools

GLAZIERS AND GROZIERS
Most glass came to the glass painters, or glaziers, from countryside kilns. It was already coloured, and the glaziers cut and shaped the glass pieces. They could vary the colours by scraping away the surface or by painting it with enamels.

Line of sketch, or cartoon

Soldered joint

THE WHOLE PICTURE
Like a fragile and beautiful jigsaw puzzle, the stained glass pieces are fitted together with the lead. The glass slots into grooves in each side of the lead strips, and the whole assembly is held firm with large horseshoe nails. Finally, the joints between the strips are soldered back and front, and putty is applied to seal in the glass. The completed panel is then set with others into the delicate stone tracery (p. 53) of a window. The lead will last for over 100 years before it needs replacing.

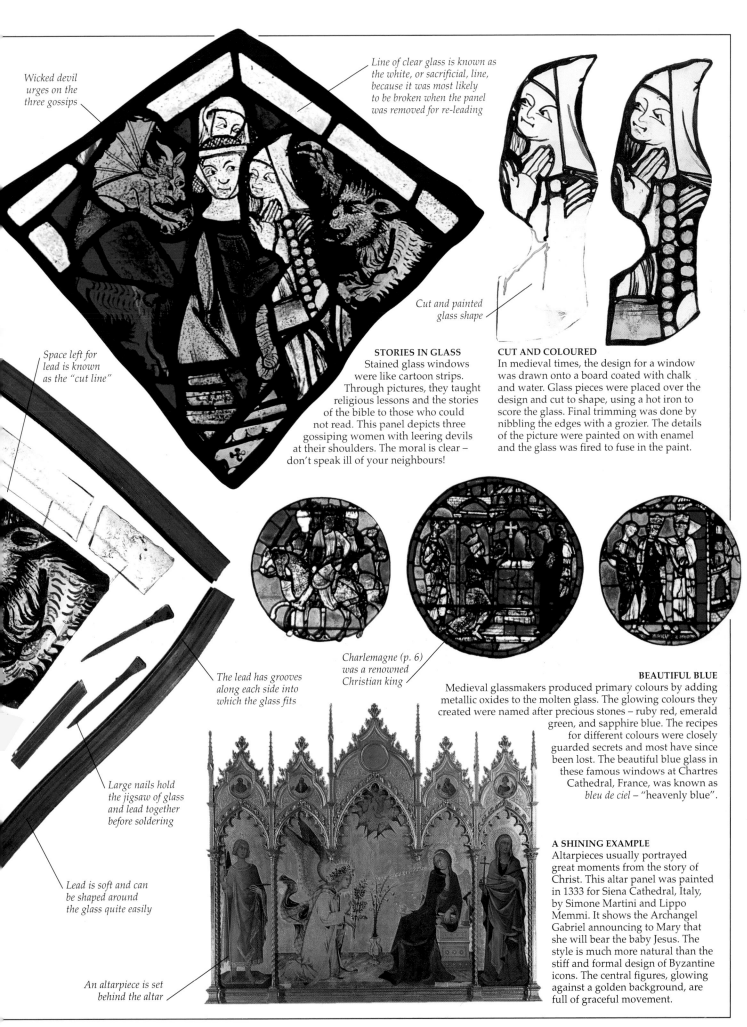

Wicked devil urges on the three gossips

Line of clear glass is known as the white, or sacrificial, line, because it was most likely to be broken when the panel was removed for re-leading

Cut and painted glass shape

Space left for lead is known as the "cut line"

STORIES IN GLASS
Stained glass windows were like cartoon strips. Through pictures, they taught religious lessons and the stories of the bible to those who could not read. This panel depicts three gossiping women with leering devils at their shoulders. The moral is clear – don't speak ill of your neighbours!

CUT AND COLOURED
In medieval times, the design for a window was drawn onto a board coated with chalk and water. Glass pieces were placed over the design and cut to shape, using a hot iron to score the glass. Final trimming was done by nibbling the edges with a grozier. The details of the picture were painted on with enamel and the glass was fired to fuse in the paint.

The lead has grooves along each side into which the glass fits

Charlemagne (p. 6) was a renowned Christian king

BEAUTIFUL BLUE
Medieval glassmakers produced primary colours by adding metallic oxides to the molten glass. The glowing colours they created were named after precious stones – ruby red, emerald green, and sapphire blue. The recipes for different colours were closely guarded secrets and most have since been lost. The beautiful blue glass in these famous windows at Chartres Cathedral, France, was known as *bleu de ciel* – "heavenly blue".

Large nails hold the jigsaw of glass and lead together before soldering

Lead is soft and can be shaped around the glass quite easily

A SHINING EXAMPLE
Altarpieces usually portrayed great moments from the story of Christ. This altar panel was painted in 1333 for Siena Cathedral, Italy, by Simone Martini and Lippo Memmi. It shows the Archangel Gabriel announcing to Mary that she will bear the baby Jesus. The style is much more natural than the stiff and formal design of Byzantine icons. The central figures, glowing against a golden background, are full of graceful movement.

An altarpiece is set behind the altar

Holy orders

"WE MUST FORM A SCHOOL IN THE LORD'S SERVICE", wrote St Benedict in the sixth century. He founded a monastery at Monte Cassino in Italy where monks could live, work, and pray together. The monks became known as the Benedictines because they followed St Benedict's "Rule" which instructed them to make three vows – of poverty (to own no property), chastity (never to marry), and obedience (to obey the orders of their leaders). Making these vows was a serious undertaking, so St Benedict ordered that every newcomer, or novice, should live in the monastery for a year before committing himself. Once he had made his vows, a novice had the crown of his head shaved in a tonsure and became a brother of the order. In time, monasteries and convents throughout Europe adopted St Benedict's Rule.

12th-century Celtic monk

Bone stylus

Wax tablet on a horn base

WAX COPY BOOK
Monks spent a lot of time copying out prayers and psalms by hand. They often wrote on wax tablets with a scratcher, or stylus. Copying holy passages was also a way of serving God. St Bernard (1090–1153) told monks, "Every word you write is a blow that smites the devil".

Tonsure

THE HISTORY MAN
Many monks were well educated and monasteries became centres of learning. St Bede (c. 673–735), also known as the Venerable Bede, was an English Benedictine monk who devoted his life to writing and scholarship. He wrote books on science, religion, and history, including the great *Ecclesiastical History of the English Nation*. Without monks like Bede, we would know much less about the history of the Middle Ages.

NO LIGHT IN THE DARKNESS
St Benedict's Rule allowed for basic comforts, but life in a monastery was never easy. At first, monks were not allowed candles for reading at services – they had to learn all the prayers, psalms, and other forms of worship by heart.

OUT OF ORDER
By the tenth century, many religious houses had become too relaxed. The monk below has been placed in the stocks with his mistress as a punishment for an illicit affair. Some French monks thought that the ideals of St Benedict were being forgotten and formed a new order at Cluny in 910. The Cluniacs tried to follow the strict and simple rules laid down by St Benedict. Other new orders were the Carthusians, who believed in a life of silent prayer, and the Cistercians, who thought that hard work was the best way to serve God.

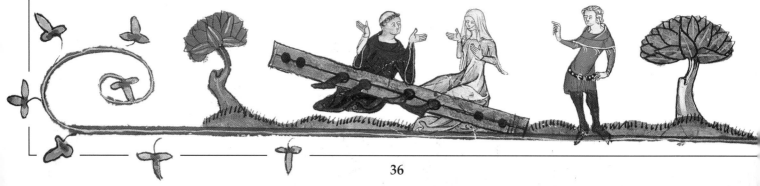

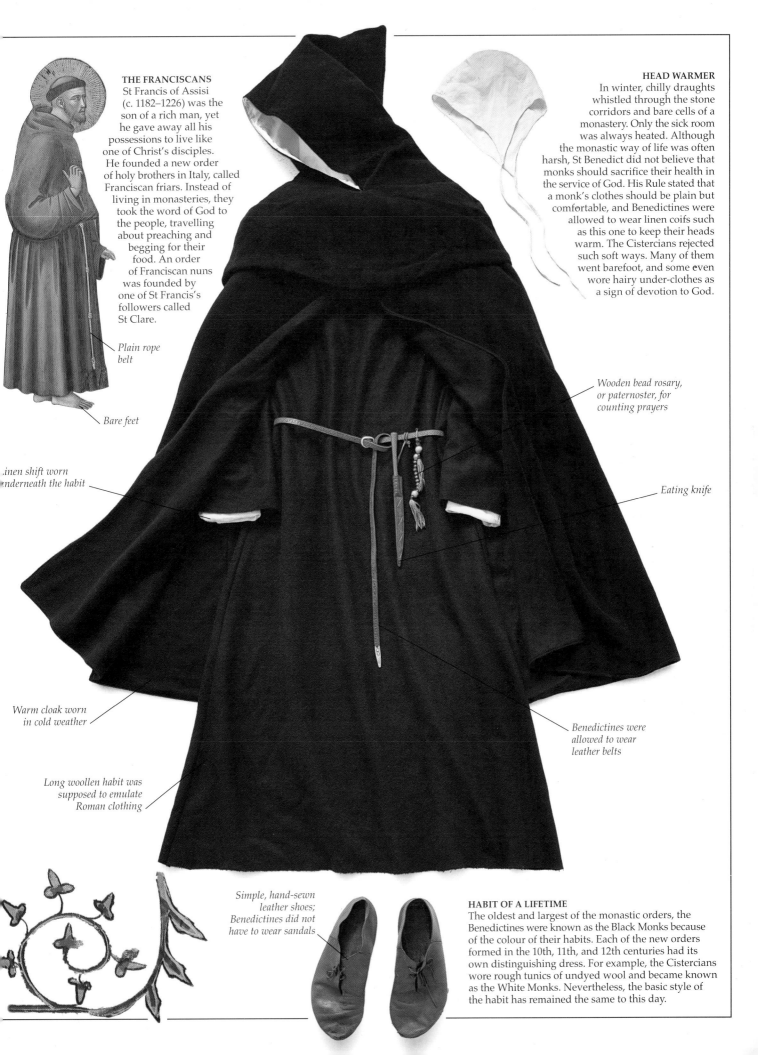

THE FRANCISCANS
St Francis of Assisi (c. 1182–1226) was the son of a rich man, yet he gave away all his possessions to live like one of Christ's disciples. He founded a new order of holy brothers in Italy, called Franciscan friars. Instead of living in monasteries, they took the word of God to the people, travelling about preaching and begging for their food. An order of Franciscan nuns was founded by one of St Francis's followers called St Clare.

Plain rope belt

Bare feet

Linen shift worn underneath the habit

Warm cloak worn in cold weather

Long woollen habit was supposed to emulate Roman clothing

HEAD WARMER
In winter, chilly draughts whistled through the stone corridors and bare cells of a monastery. Only the sick room was always heated. Although the monastic way of life was often harsh, St Benedict did not believe that monks should sacrifice their health in the service of God. His Rule stated that a monk's clothes should be plain but comfortable, and Benedictines were allowed to wear linen coifs such as this one to keep their heads warm. The Cistercians rejected such soft ways. Many of them went barefoot, and some even wore hairy under-clothes as a sign of devotion to God.

Wooden bead rosary, or paternoster, for counting prayers

Eating knife

Benedictines were allowed to wear leather belts

Simple, hand-sewn leather shoes; Benedictines did not have to wear sandals

HABIT OF A LIFETIME
The oldest and largest of the monastic orders, the Benedictines are known as the Black Monks because of the colour of their habits. Each of the new orders formed in the 10th, 11th, and 12th centuries had its own distinguishing dress. For example, the Cistercians wore rough tunics of undyed wool and became known as the White Monks. Nevertheless, the basic style of the habit has remained the same to this day.

Life in a monastery

MONASTERIES AND CONVENTS were worlds of their own. Ruled by an abbot or an abbess, they were cut off from society and governed by special rules. When novices (p. 36) entered a holy order, they were expected to stay there for the rest of their lives. From that moment on, every part of each day was accounted for. Much of the time was spent attending the eight daily church services and reading or copying religious texts. Other duties included caring for the poor and sick, teaching younger members of the order, or tending to the gardens, fishponds, mill, and farm. There was a general rule of silence in most religious houses and daily tasks had to be carried out without speaking. Although they lived apart from society, monks and nuns served an important role in the community. They provided food for the poor, care for the sick, and accommodation for pilgrims and other travellers.

ROUND OF PRAYERS
Monks went to the monastery church eight times a day in an unchanging round of services, or offices. The first, Matins, began at two o'clock in the morning and dormitories were built near the church so that the monks wouldn't be late for services. In the early 11th century, monks at Canterbury, England, had to sing 55 psalms, one after the other, and all without sitting down. The Benedictines shown here at least have pews to rest on.

Straw "hackle", or jacket placed over the hive in winter to keep the bees warm

Statue of Mary and Jesus

Single-chambered wicker beehive daubed with clay

Wicker beehive made from woven willow or hazel

Abbey church

BUSY BEES
The Cistercians (p. 36) believed that performing hard manual labour was the best way to lead a holy life. They built large monasteries in remote rural areas where they could farm the land in peace. Their estates grew so big that lay brothers (those who had taken holy vows but lacked the education to become monks) were taken on to help. Most monasteries had to produce their own food. These beehives, or skeps, provided honey to eat and wax for candles.

CARE IN A CONVENT
Nuns took the same vows as monks (p. 36) and lived in much the same way. Devoted to serving the poor, most convents and monasteries ran hospitals to care for the sick. These were open to all, and nuns and monks were instructed to, "Receive the patients as you would Christ Himself". The medicines and treatments may have been primitive (pp. 60–61), but at least patients were given food and a clean bed. Without the work of the Church, there would have been very little health care in the Middle Ages.

Model of an abbey in the 15th century

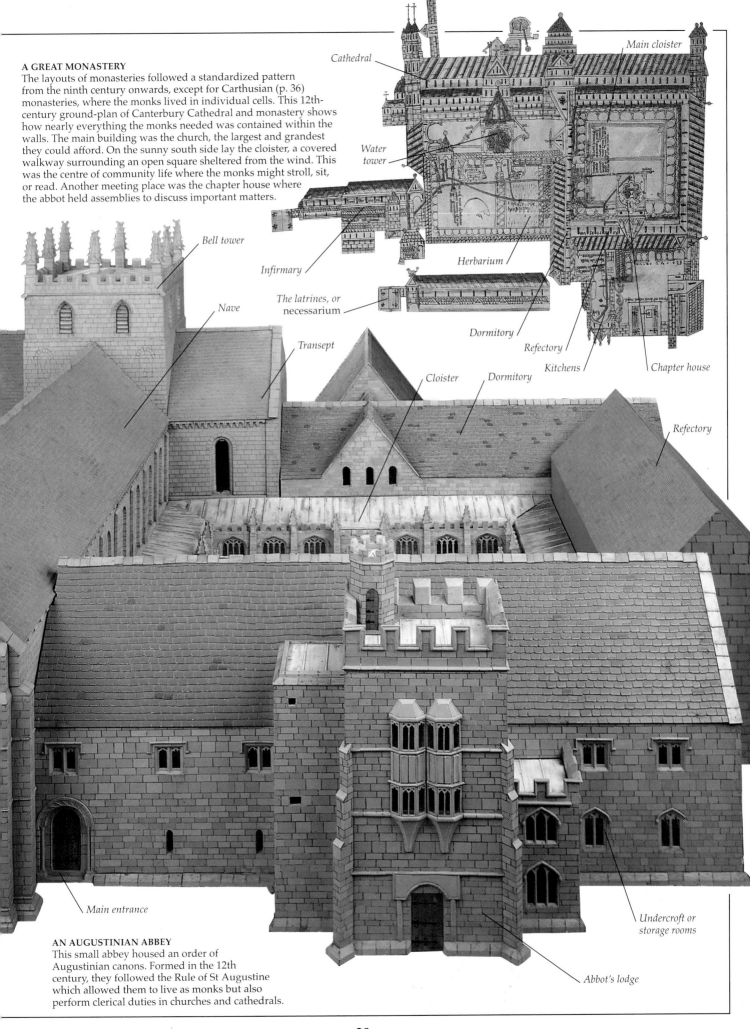

A GREAT MONASTERY

The layouts of monasteries followed a standardized pattern from the ninth century onwards, except for Carthusian (p. 36) monasteries, where the monks lived in individual cells. This 12th-century ground-plan of Canterbury Cathedral and monastery shows how nearly everything the monks needed was contained within the walls. The main building was the church, the largest and grandest they could afford. On the sunny south side lay the cloister, a covered walkway surrounding an open square sheltered from the wind. This was the centre of community life where the monks might stroll, sit, or read. Another meeting place was the chapter house where the abbot held assemblies to discuss important matters.

Cathedral

Main cloister

Water tower

Infirmary

Herbarium

The latrines, or necessarium

Dormitory

Refectory

Kitchens

Chapter house

Bell tower

Nave

Transept

Cloister

Dormitory

Refectory

Main entrance

Undercroft or storage rooms

Abbot's lodge

AN AUGUSTINIAN ABBEY

This small abbey housed an order of Augustinian canons. Formed in the 12th century, they followed the Rule of St Augustine which allowed them to live as monks but also perform clerical duties in churches and cathedrals.

The written word

UNTIL 1100 BOOKS WERE RARE and were usually found only in monastery libraries. Everything was written by hand and monks spent many hours in the "scriptorium" copying out religious texts. A long manuscript such as the bible might take one scribe a year to complete. As a way of glorifying God, many manuscripts were beautifully decorated, or illuminated, with jewel-like paints and precious gold leaf. After 1200, books became more common, especially when the first universities opened in Paris and Bologna. Professional scribes and illuminators began to produce books as well as the monks, often making copies to order for wealthy customers. Personal books of psalms, called psalters, became popular among the aristocracy.

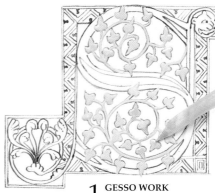

1 GESSO WORK
One of the most striking features of medieval manuscripts are the beautifully decorated capital letters that begin each page. Painted in vibrant colours, they were often gilded with gold leaf to make them even brighter. The first stage of illuminating a letter is applying the gesso, a kind of glue made from plaster, white lead, water, sugar, and egg-white, which makes a sticky surface for the gold.

The gold leaf only sticks to the moist gesso

The moulded gesso gives a 3-D effect to the gilded leaves

Each leaf is burnished separately

3 BURNISHED BRIGHT
Once the gold leaf has set into the gesso, the illuminator rubs, or burnishes, it to make it shiny. The traditional burnishing tool was a dog's or wolf's tooth attached to a wooden handle. Finally, the rest of the background is carefully painted in around the gilding.

2 GILDING THE LETTER
The gesso is left to set over night, and the next day the illuminator smooths any rough edges and breathes on the gesso to make it slightly moist. He then lays a sheet of gold leaf over the gesso, covers it with a silk cloth and presses it firmly onto the glue. The surplus gold is removed with a soft brush.

SCRIBES AND SCHOLARS
However hard scribes worked, books remained scarce. Few people could afford to buy them, and scholars had to travel around monastic libraries to study the texts they wanted. This statue of a scholar is from Chartres Cathedral, France.

4 SHINING THROUGH THE AGES
The finished letter is like a tiny work of art. Apart from leaves and flowers, many illuminated initials contain pictures of people and animals. If the gold is properly burnished it will never fade – most medieval manuscripts still shine brightly today.

Curling leaves are a popular "Gothic" design

Bone spectacles

SIGHT FOR SORE EYES
Hours of close copying often damaged the eyesight. Europeans first started wearing spectacles in the 13th century. The invention of printing in the 1450s (p. 62) made more books available, and the sale of spectacles rocketed.

The paternoster, or Lord's prayer, written in Latin

Feather is rarely left on the quill because it gets in the way

Inkwell slots into a hole in the desk

Horn "book" hangs from a belt

Point used for pricking outlines on parchment

Stylus   Goose quills   Horn inkwells

A LITTLE LEARNING
Most schooling in the Middle Ages took place in monasteries, convents, and cathedrals. Children (mostly boys who were destined for holy orders) received a basic education in reading and writing, and spent much of their time learning prayers and bible passages by heart – all in Latin. They were often forbidden to talk or play, and were beaten with a birch rod when their attention wandered!

FIRST LESSONS
Children began learning to read with a horn book such as this, first used in the 1450s. The alphabet or prayer was covered with a transparent sheet of horn to protect it from grubby fingers.

Selection of quills

Sloping desk

Straight-backed chair made from white ash wood

Jug of ale or weak wine for refreshment

Drinking vessel

Horn books to copy from

Table-top folds backwards

SEAT FOR A SCRIBE
A scribe might sit for hours at his work copying out Latin texts in beautiful, well-formed script. He rested his parchment on a sloping desk, which made it easier to hold his pen at right angles (quills wrote best this way). In his left hand, he held a pen-knife, which he used to hold down the page, to scrape out mistakes, and to sharpen his quill – often up to 60 times a day.

Folding table, or tabula plicata, can be stored flat against a wall

Decoration carved only on the side that faces the room

Cushion made long hours of work more comfortable

"Turned" chair-leg decorated with bands of vermilion paint

Saints and pilgrims

Most people in the Middle Ages hoped to go on a pilgrimage to a holy shrine at some point in their lives. They went for many reasons – as proof of their devotion to God, as an act of penance for their sins, or to find a cure for an illness. The holy city of Jerusalem was a favourite destination, as were Rome, where both St Peter and St Paul were believed to be buried, the shrine of St James at Santiago de Compostela in Spain, and Canterbury Cathedral in England. On the road, rich and poor travelled together and, for many, pilgrimages were a sort of holiday. To pass the time, people sang songs and hymns, played pipes, and told stories over their evening meals in roadside taverns.

ON THE ROAD
In the early Middle Ages, most pilgrims travelled on foot. They wore long woollen tunics, called sclaveins, broad-brimmed felt hats, and sandals.

Front part of reliquary contains a holy cross set in pearls and rock crystal

Pewter badge of St Thomas Becket

Tiny flask, or ampulla, for holy water

Scallop shell emblem of Santiago de Compostela

SIGN OF THE SHRINE
Like modern tourists, medieval pilgrims often sported badges to show that they had been to a certain shrine. They wore them on their hats to make it clear that they were on a holy journey and had the right to protection. The scallop shell was a popular emblem.

PORTABLE RELICS
Holy relics, or the bones of saints, were not only kept in shrines. People carried them in bags around their necks or in beautifully decorated cases like this one. Knights often had relics placed in their sword hilts.

Back part of reliquary contains pieces of bone, or relics, set in gold as a sign of their value

Figure of Christ

Becket's body is laid in a shroud

Becket is carried to Heaven by angels

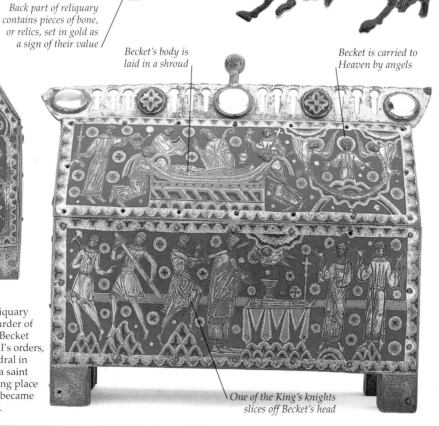

A MARTYR'S BONES
This 12th-century reliquary casket depicts the murder of Archbishop Thomas Becket (1118–70), on Henry II's orders, in Canterbury Cathedral in 1170. Becket became a saint and Canterbury, resting place of his bones, quickly became a place of pilgrimage.

One of the King's knights slices off Becket's head

THE PILGRIM'S POET
Geoffrey Chaucer (c. 1340–1400) wrote the best-loved book about pilgrims, *The Canterbury Tales*. It is a series of stories in verse told by a party of 30 pilgrims to pass the time as they ride to Canterbury. The pilgrims, who include a knight, a miller, a friar, a prioress, and a cook, portray a vivid and often hilarious picture of medieval life.

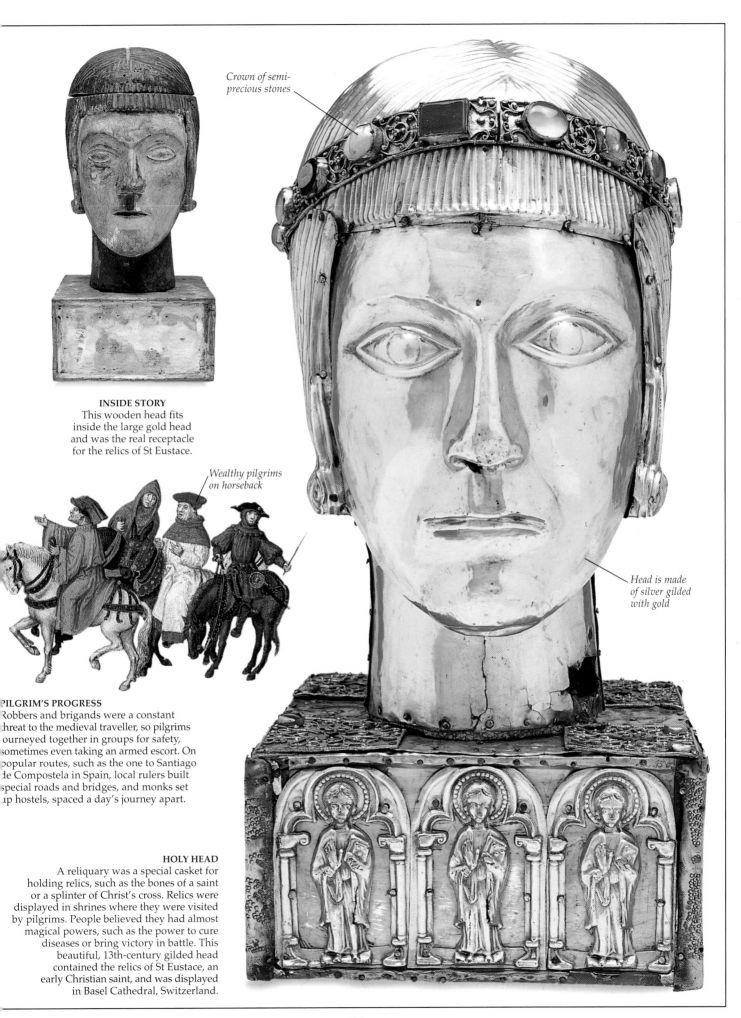

INSIDE STORY
This wooden head fits inside the large gold head and was the real receptacle for the relics of St Eustace.

Crown of semi-precious stones

Wealthy pilgrims on horseback

Head is made of silver gilded with gold

PILGRIM'S PROGRESS
Robbers and brigands were a constant threat to the medieval traveller, so pilgrims journeyed together in groups for safety, sometimes even taking an armed escort. On popular routes, such as the one to Santiago de Compostela in Spain, local rulers built special roads and bridges, and monks set up hostels, spaced a day's journey apart.

HOLY HEAD
A reliquary was a special casket for holding relics, such as the bones of a saint or a splinter of Christ's cross. Relics were displayed in shrines where they were visited by pilgrims. People believed they had almost magical powers, such as the power to cure diseases or bring victory in battle. This beautiful, 13th-century gilded head contained the relics of St Eustace, an early Christian saint, and was displayed in Basel Cathedral, Switzerland.

The Islamic world

MUHAMMAD THE PROPHET of Islam died in 632. Within 100 years a great Islamic civilization had developed and Arab armies had conquered a vast empire that stretched from Spain and North Africa to Persia and India. International trade flourished in the Islamic world, spreading ideas as well as goods. Muslim scientists became particularly advanced in the fields of medicine and mathematics: they were skilled surgeons and eye-doctors, invented algebra (from the Arabic *al-jebr*) and introduced the Arabic numeral system to Europe, a version of which is still in use today. Although the Christians saw the Muslims as an "infidel" race and an almost inhuman enemy during the Crusades, as trade links grew stronger, they learned much from this highly advanced civilization.

GLITTERING PRIZE
The rich cities of the Islamic world were prime targets for the plundering crusaders (p. 28). In 1099, they succeeded in overrunning the holy city of Jerusalem, killing its inhabitants and pillaging its vast treasures (above).

Inlaid decoration

Traditional Arabic pattern

MUSLIM MARVELS
The lute almost came to symbolize medieval European music, but its true origin was in the Islamic world, where it was known as *al-'ud*. Many Muslim rulers, or caliphs, were great patrons of art and learning, and fostered the work of musicians, poets, artists, and scholars at their courts. The lute was just one of many inventions and ideas that came to Europe from the Muslim empire.

HEAVENLY GUIDANCE
The Muslims were brilliant astronomers. They developed the astrolabe which enabled travellers to fix their position by studying the night sky. Camel drivers used this instrument to navigate across the desert, and Europeans soon copied the idea and used it for finding their way at sea.

LUXURY TRAIN
Camel trains carried a huge range of goods across the deserts and mountains of the Islamic world. In the dazzling bazaars of Baghdad and Damascus, the wealthy could buy a stunning variety of luxury goods, from Persian carpets and African ivory, to Asian silks, spices, jewels, and furs.

HERO OF A HOLY WAR
Saladin (1137–1193) was a great Islamic sultan who led the Muslim armies against the crusaders, and recaptured Jerusalem. He was respected even by his enemies as a brilliant general and a wise man.

MEDICINE MEN
Even as the Crusades were raging, Europeans learned a great deal from Islamic doctors, whose knowledge was far in advance of their own. Cures for numerous ills could be bought in apothecaries such as this. In the 11th century, the great Arab doctor Avicenna (980–1037) wrote a medical encyclopedia that became the single greatest influence on medieval medicine.

ARTS AND CRAFTS
Islamic craftsmen were renowned for their beautiful enamel work. They usually decorated religious artefacts, such as this 13th-century mosque lamp, with Arabic words and geometric patterns because Islamic tradition banned images of human figures and other living things from religious buildings.

Trade and commerce

THE EARLIEST MEDIEVAL MERCHANTS were pedlars who sold goods to villages and towns. By the 12th century, Europe had grown more prosperous and more goods were produced. Merchants were no longer simply wandering adventurers. They became dealers, employers, and ship-owners, sending their carriers along a network of trade routes linking the European cities. By 1300, cargo ships from Genoa and Venice in Italy were taking precious metals, silks, and other luxuries from the eastern Mediterranean out to England and Flanders (Belgium). There they picked up wool, coal, and timber for the return voyage. German and Dutch ships took iron, copper, and lead south to the Mediterranean, and brought back wine, oil, and salt.

CANDLE WAX
This tiny candle was used to melt the wax for sealing letters and documents.

BALANCING THE BOOKS
Merchants needed to keep careful accounts of their money. Traders in 14th-century Florence developed a system of double-entry book-keeping. Each deal was recorded in two ledgers – one for credits, the other for debits. The amounts in each ledger should always balance.

Horn inkwell and quill

Quills were trimmed before use

One half of a tally stick

TALLY STICK
A debt could be recorded on a tally stick. Notches were cut into it to record the amount, then the stick was split in two and each party kept half. When the debt was settled, the tally was destroyed or kept as a record.

KEEP THE CHANGE
Merchants kept small numbers of coins in money boxes like this. Most coins were silver, but in 1252, the city of Florence minted the first gold coins since Roman times – the golden florin.

14th-century document seal

SIGNED AND SEALED
As trading methods grew more complex, much more paperwork was needed. Merchants had to employ clerks and scribes to help them. There were letters giving details of business deals, bills of sale, orders, contracts to suppliers, and documents promising payment. All of these had to be signed and marked with the wax seals of the merchants involved.

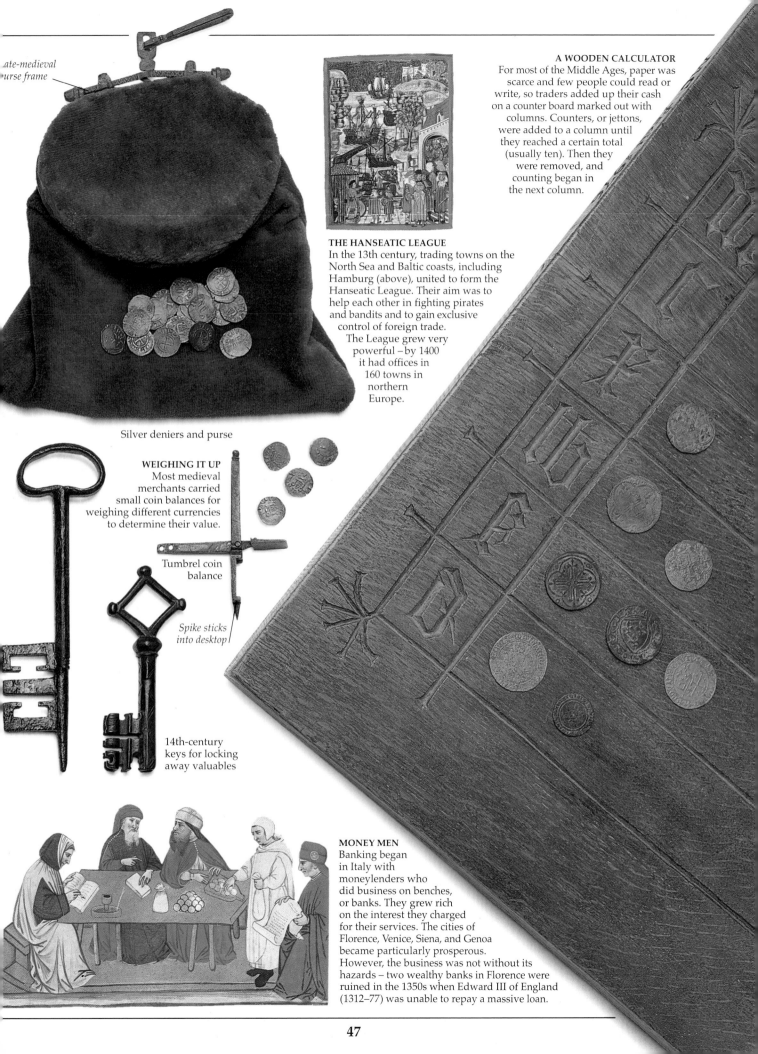

Late-medieval purse frame

A WOODEN CALCULATOR

For most of the Middle Ages, paper was scarce and few people could read or write, so traders added up their cash on a counter board marked out with columns. Counters, or jettons, were added to a column until they reached a certain total (usually ten). Then they were removed, and counting began in the next column.

THE HANSEATIC LEAGUE

In the 13th century, trading towns on the North Sea and Baltic coasts, including Hamburg (above), united to form the Hanseatic League. Their aim was to help each other in fighting pirates and bandits and to gain exclusive control of foreign trade. The League grew very powerful – by 1400 it had offices in 160 towns in northern Europe.

Silver deniers and purse

WEIGHING IT UP

Most medieval merchants carried small coin balances for weighing different currencies to determine their value.

Tumbrel coin balance

Spike sticks into desktop

14th-century keys for locking away valuables

MONEY MEN

Banking began in Italy with moneylenders who did business on benches, or banks. They grew rich on the interest they charged for their services. The cities of Florence, Venice, Siena, and Genoa became particularly prosperous. However, the business was not without its hazards – two wealthy banks in Florence were ruined in the 1350s when Edward III of England (1312–77) was unable to repay a massive loan.

Life in the town

As TRADE GREW, so did towns. At first they were part of a lord's or king's domain, but as they became wealthier, townsmen resented having to work for someone else. In northern France there were violent scenes as towns struggled to become independent "communes". In England the process was more peaceful. Town-dwellers agreed to pay a fixed sum each year in return for a royal charter which granted them the right to govern themselves. The town then became a free "borough" with the power to make its own laws, form trade guilds (p. 50), and raise taxes. The people also became free citizens, or burgesses.

THE NIGHT WATCH
At sunset, the town bells rang to sound the curfew. This meant that everyone had to finish work and go home. There were no street lights in medieval towns, and they could be dangerous places after dark. Nightwatchmen patrolled the streets with lanterns to deter criminals.

STREET SIGNS
Towns were first and foremost centres of trade with bustling streets full of shops. Since few people could read, many shops advertised their wares by hanging out a symbol of their trade, such as a loaf for a baker or a basin for a barber (seen in the middle of the picture). In some towns, traders or craftsmen of the same type had shops in the same street, so shoemakers worked in Shoe Lane, tailors on Threadneedle Street, fishmongers in the Rue de la Poissonerie, and so on.

15th-century French city

WALLED IN
Medieval towns were surrounded by strong stone walls. These were not only to keep out villains. They also made sure that merchants and other visitors could only enter by the gates, where they had to pay a toll. Town gates were opened at dawn and locked at dusk.

THE LORD MAYOR
Most towns were governed by an elected mayor and a local council. Mayors became powerful figures who were often courted by lords and kings. Some even loaned money to the monarch. Dick Whittington (c. 1358–1423) was a famous English mayor. The son of a knight, he became a wealthy merchant and was elected Lord Mayor of London three times.

TOWERS THAT BE
Powerful families struggled to gain control of the new communes and boroughs. In Italy, they built defensive towers as symbols of their wealth and importance. At San Gimignano in Tuscany, over 70 towers were erected in the 12th century. Eventually, most town councils forbade any building higher than the town hall!

GARDEY LOO!
Slop pails and chamber pots were emptied out of windows with the cry "Gardey loo!" from the French *gardez l'eau* which means "Look out, water!" Town-dwellers were naturally wary when walking down the street!

"Half-moon" leather knife

Spike possibly used to make holes for stitching

Hook-like leather knife

LIVING OVER THE SHOP
Most craftsmen had their workshops on the ground floors of their homes. These also served as shops, and finished goods were displayed on a hinged shelf at the front. In the evening, shutters were pulled down for security. The shopkeeper usually had a storeroom at the back, and he and his family lived on the floors above. This 15th-century building is divided into two shops. Only the smaller shop on the right has access to the upper floors, which means that the other was probably rented out to another business.

Upper storeys were home to the shopkeeper's family

A staircase at the rear leads to the upper chambers

Sole made from tough cattle hide

Waxed linen thread

Upper made from goatskin, which is strong and flexible

Half-finished shoe will be turned other way out when complete

TOWN TRADE
Craftsmen such as shoemakers worked at windows that opened onto the street, giving them the opportunity to show off their skills to passers-by. Medieval shoemakers were known as cordwainers after the best shoe-leather from Cordoba in Spain. These long-toed "poulaine" shoes were fashionable in the late 14th century and would have been sold to a wealthy merchant or burgess.

LEAN STREETS
There was a limited amount of space within the walls of a medieval town, and houses were built very close together. To maximise space, the upper storeys of buildings were jettied, or built jutting out above the ground floors. In some places, the houses on either side almost touched each other, making some streets quite gloomy and airless.

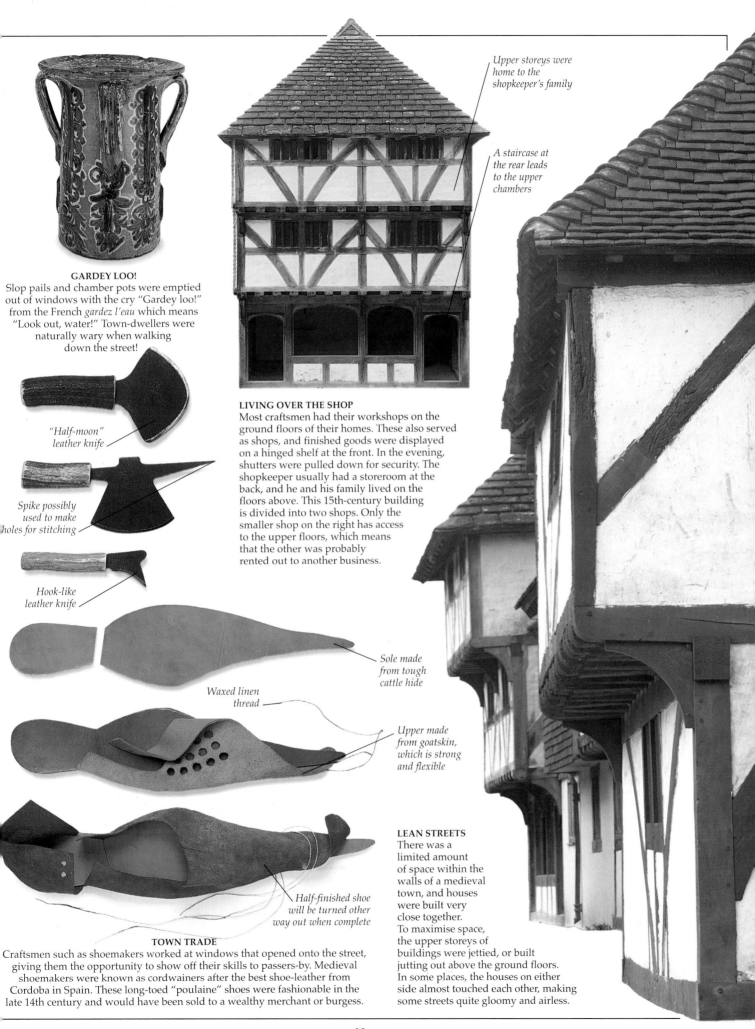

The guild masters

In 1262, A BOOK OF TRADES compiled in Paris listed over 100 different crafts, each of which had its own association, or guild. By the 1420's, guilds existed in most big towns throughout Europe and their numbers were still growing. Their main object was to gain high wages and exclusive control of their business for their members. They fixed prices and standards of work, and made sure that no outsiders competed with them. Guilds also supported members who fell on hard times, providing them with money from a central fund. In time, the guilds grew rich and powerful. They built grand guildhalls, paraded in fine livery on special occasions, and often played an important role in civic affairs.

THE ARMOURERS
The Armourers' Guild maintained the standards of the craftsmen who made plate armour. Near Milan in Italy, one of the centres of armour-making in the 15th century, whole villages were employed in the trade.

WOMEN AT WORK
Most guilds would not allow women members, but this did not prevent women from learning skilled trades. Many worked with their husbands or fathers. Silk-weaving in London was almost entirely done by women, although they were not allowed to form their own guild.

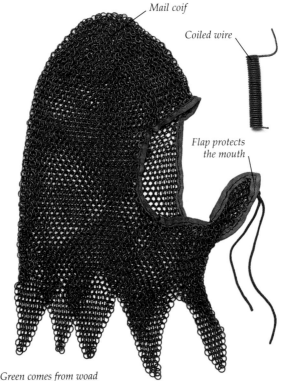

Mail coif

Coiled wire

Flap protects the mouth

Rings snipped off wire

Rivets

Each ring end is flattened and linked by a rivet

ANOTHER FINE MESH
Mail-making was a skilled and painstaking process. Each ring was linked to four others and held together by a tiny rivet. An entire suit of mail could be made up of thousands of rings.

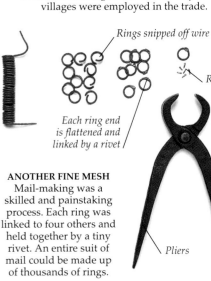

Pliers

Green comes from woad leaves and weld

Blue produced by woad or indigo dyes

Linen dyed with madder root

Bright orange and red dyes come from madder roots

Oak bark gives a brown colour

Yellow comes from dyers' green weed, or weld

Plant-dyed wools

MASTER DYERS
In the Middle Ages cloth-making was a gigantic industry that employed a large array of guild crafts. There were the weavers, the fullers and walkers (who cleaned and compacted the cloth), the carders (who brushed it), and the shearmen (who trimmed it). Then there were the dyers, who dyed the cloth in huge heated vats full of dyestuff (right).

GUILDHALLS
The richer guilds had chambers or guildhalls, which proudly displayed their coats of arms. Here members met for a banquet on the anniversary of their patron saint, and the guild court sat to settle disputes and punish members who had disobeyed the strict rules.

"Borrelais" hat derived from a hood worn the wrong way around

THE GUILD MASTER
This fine costume would have been worn by a middle-class merchant or business owner in the 1400s. Towards the end of the Middle Ages, the wealthier merchants began to control the guilds' affairs for their own ends. They bought the raw materials and sold the finished goods, and were more interested in making money than in the welfare of the poorer tradesmen. Guild masters also became important civic figures who often had the final say in the election of the town mayor.

Fashionable fur-trimmed sleeves

LEARNING A TRADE
Getting to the top of a guild was a long and hard process. An apprentice had to pay a large sum of money just to start. His apprenticeship lasted about seven years, during which he learned every aspect of the craft from a master (seen here judging work by a mason and a carpenter). After this, he became a journeyman (from the French *journée*, or "day") and worked for a daily wage. A journeyman could one day become a master – as long as he paid the right fees.

Decorated leather purse

Personal eating knife

Blue woollen doublet lined with linen

Fine woollen coat made with a large amount of material as a sign of wealth

The codpiece, which served as a fly, became fashionable after 1450

Expensive mid-calf leather boots

"Joined" hose were made to measure

Emblem of the Shoemakers' Guild

51

The stonemasons

OF ALL MEDIEVAL CRAFTSMEN, skilled masons were the most highly paid and respected. It was they who built the great cathedrals and castles that still rise above our towns and cities. Before they formed exclusive guilds (pp. 50–51) in the 14th century, masons organized their trade from their lodges. These were the masons' headquarters on the building site where they worked under cover in bad weather, ate their meals, and discussed trade secrets. Rules and working conditions were set out by the lodge leaders. Masons learned their craft on the site itself, often serving an apprenticeship of up to seven years. The most talented might go on to become master masons, with the responsibility for designing and overseeing the building of an entire cathedral.

"Stock" rests on top of the stone

Blade measures depth

SINKING SQUARE
Each stone had to be worked precisely to shape before being hoisted into position. The sinking square was used to measure the depth of holes or grooves and to check that the corners were square.

SCORING A CURVE
The mason had to mark out his stone to show him where to cut or carve. To mark a curved line parallel to the edge he used a box trammel. Holding the wooden handle firmly against the edge, he dragged it along. The trammel point moved across the stone, scoring a line.

Sharp point scores the stone

SQUARED UP
The square was one of the mason's most important tools. It was used for making sure corners were straight.

Well-worn chisel-head

Pitching tool for making clean breaks in rough stone

PITCHER THIS
Every single stone in a cathedral would have taken about a day to cut and finish. Because it was heavy and expensive to transport, the stone was cut approximately to size at the quarry. At the building site, the mason's first job was to finish cutting the rough stone with a big curved saw. Then he used a hammer, a heavy, blunt chisel called a pitching tool, and a punch (right) to chip off the larger lumps and produce nearly straight edges.

Hammer-headed chisels

Punch for chipping off large bits of stone

HEAVY LUMP
The lump hammer was used for hitting hammer-headed chisels in the rough shaping work. The softer the stone, the heavier the hammer.

UNITED BY DIVIDERS
Dividers, or wing compasses, became the masons' special emblem. They were used mainly to measure a distance on a template, and then transfer the measurement to a piece of stone.

Medieval dividers

Template for the cross-section of the joint

Joint

Paper template for a piece of window tracery

Modern masons mark out a block with pencil lines

MARKING OUT
The mason selected a block of stone that had been trimmed square and smooth on which to mark out the template. He then scratched, or scribed, around the edges.

ACCORDING TO PLAN
The pattern, or template, for each stone was cut out of board, leather, or parchment and laid over the stone for the mason to copy.

Draughting chisel for carving the first outline

Gouge for working curved surfaces

Claw chisel for scraping away stone

Mallet-headed chisels for use with a mallet

CHOOSING A CHISEL
An apprentice mason had to learn to handle a bewildering array of chisels. Each mason owned his own tools, all of which bore his personal mark. They were usually passed down from generation to generation and the design of modern masonry tools like these has changed little since medieval times.

Stone relief (left) dedicated to the Stonemasons' Guild from the church of Or San Michele in Florence

WORKS OF ART
Some stonemasons became specialist sculptors. Intricate carvings such as the figures, foliage, and animals that decorated the great cathedrals were created by highly skilled "imaginators".

MASTER MIND
The master mason was in charge of everything on the building site, from designing the building to hiring workers and ordering stone from the quarry. His job was that of an architect and a foreman all rolled into one – he set out plans and templates for his workers, but was also expected to work alongside them on occasion.

Cusp (from the Latin cuspis which means "spearhead")

MASONS' MARK
A mason "signed" each finished stone with his personal mark to show how much work he had completed.

THE FINISHED ARTICLE
The carving of ornamental stonework such as the stone ribs, or tracery, that supported stained glass windows, took many years to master. Experienced stonemasons could carve any number of complex pieces. This section of tracery links the delicate ribs in the upper part of a window.

SHAPING THE STONE
The final shaping of the stone was the job of a banker mason who worked on a bench, or banker. Using chisels, gouges, and saws, he cut the stone to the scribed pattern.

Masons rub away tool marks on soft stone with a toothed iron plate called a cock's comb, or drag

WORKING IN THE LODGE
Outside building work was only done in the good weather of the summer months. In winter, stonemasons laboured on under cover in their lodge, designing, marking out, and cutting pieces of stone.

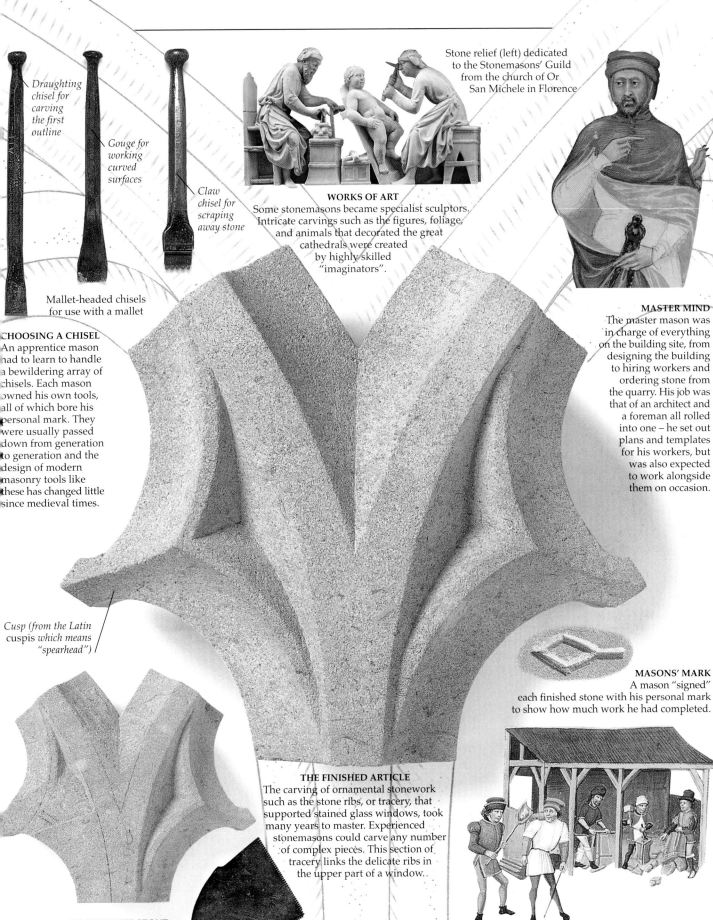

Fairs and feast days

BOTH PEASANTS AND TOWN-DWELLERS looked forward to the festivals and fairs that marked the important days of the year. On holy days, or holidays, such as Christmas and Easter, everyone took time off work to attend special church services, banquets, and festivities. Great trade fairs, often held on the feast days of saints, were also occasions for fun. Merchants came from all over Europe to buy and sell their goods and were entertained by musicians, acrobats, and players. Other special events that were related to different times of the year were May Day, Midsummer's Eve, and the Harvest Home.

NO DICE
Although it was frowned upon by the Church, gambling was one of the most widespread of medieval pastimes. People played dice games and betted on wrestling matches, cock fights, and bear baiting.

YULETIDE FOOLS
One of the highlights of Christmas was the Feast of Fools. A "bishop" was chosen and dressed up in mock vestments. He led everyone into church and recited services in gibberish. Meanwhile, others played dice on the altar and sang rude songs.

BALANCING ACT
Acrobats, jugglers, and dancing bears were all popular forms of entertainment at medieval festivals.

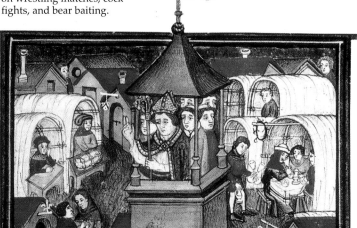

THE GREAT FAIRS
Fairs often grew out of religious festivals. After Nôtre-Dame Cathedral in Paris acquired a piece of Christ's "true cross" in 1109, thousands of pilgrims came to visit this holy relic (p. 42) each June. Merchants set up their stalls in the surrounding streets, and soon the fair had grown into a major event. The Bishop of Paris is seen here bestowing a blessing on the proceedings.

FAIR CHEWS
There was plenty of food on offer at fairs and markets. Simple baked or deep-fried meat pies like these "chewets" were the most common fare.

OUT ON THE TOWN
Many people came to fairs simply to have a good time and tavern keepers did a roaring trade. Large amounts of cheap ale and wine were consumed and drunkenness was common! In this Italian tavern, fresh quantities of wine are being passed up from the cellar to supply the carousing merchants.

Canvas
cover

New pattens
(p. 23) for sale

Leather
costrel
(p. 11)

Leather
tankards

AT THE MARKET
Besides the great fairs,
there were weekly markets
in most big towns. Pedlars,
merchants, drovers of cattle,
sheep, pigs, and even geese,
all came. Stalls sold a huge
array of goods from cheese,
eggs, and salt, to pots and
pans, tools, knives, shoes,
and cloth. This reconstructed
medieval market stall
contains leather goods
that would have been
on sale at markets in the
14th and 15th centuries.

Coloured
goatskin
for making
shoes

Large roll of
cattlehide for shoe
soles (p. 49)

Wooden frame can
be easily folded up
for transporting
the stall

Wooden shoe
"lasts" for
shoemaking

Leather
bottles

Old shoes waiting
to be mended

Left-over leather from
cut-out shoe patterns

Medieval music

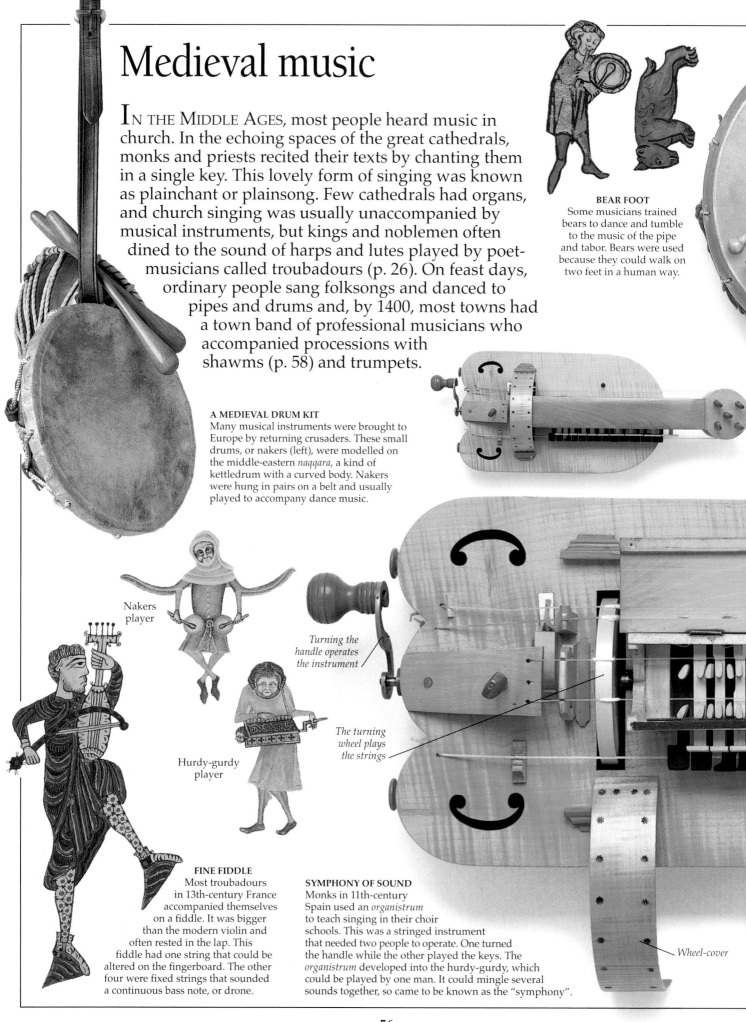

IN THE MIDDLE AGES, most people heard music in church. In the echoing spaces of the great cathedrals, monks and priests recited their texts by chanting them in a single key. This lovely form of singing was known as plainchant or plainsong. Few cathedrals had organs, and church singing was usually unaccompanied by musical instruments, but kings and noblemen often dined to the sound of harps and lutes played by poet-musicians called troubadours (p. 26). On feast days, ordinary people sang folksongs and danced to pipes and drums and, by 1400, most towns had a town band of professional musicians who accompanied processions with shawms (p. 58) and trumpets.

BEAR FOOT
Some musicians trained bears to dance and tumble to the music of the pipe and tabor. Bears were used because they could walk on two feet in a human way.

A MEDIEVAL DRUM KIT
Many musical instruments were brought to Europe by returning crusaders. These small drums, or nakers (left), were modelled on the middle-eastern *naqqara*, a kind of kettledrum with a curved body. Nakers were hung in pairs on a belt and usually played to accompany dance music.

Nakers player

Turning the handle operates the instrument

The turning wheel plays the strings

Hurdy-gurdy player

FINE FIDDLE
Most troubadours in 13th-century France accompanied themselves on a fiddle. It was bigger than the modern violin and often rested in the lap. This fiddle had one string that could be altered on the fingerboard. The other four were fixed strings that sounded a continuous bass note, or drone.

SYMPHONY OF SOUND
Monks in 11th-century Spain used an *organistrum* to teach singing in their choir schools. This was a stringed instrument that needed two people to operate. One turned the handle while the other played the keys. The *organistrum* developed into the hurdy-gurdy, which could be played by one man. It could mingle several sounds together, so came to be known as the "symphony".

Wheel-cover

Drumstick

Pipe

ONE MAN BAND
The smallest of all dance bands was the pipe and tabor. The pipe had only three holes, and the musician could easily play it with his left hand, while hitting the tabor with his right. These simple instruments were commonly used to accompany village dances.

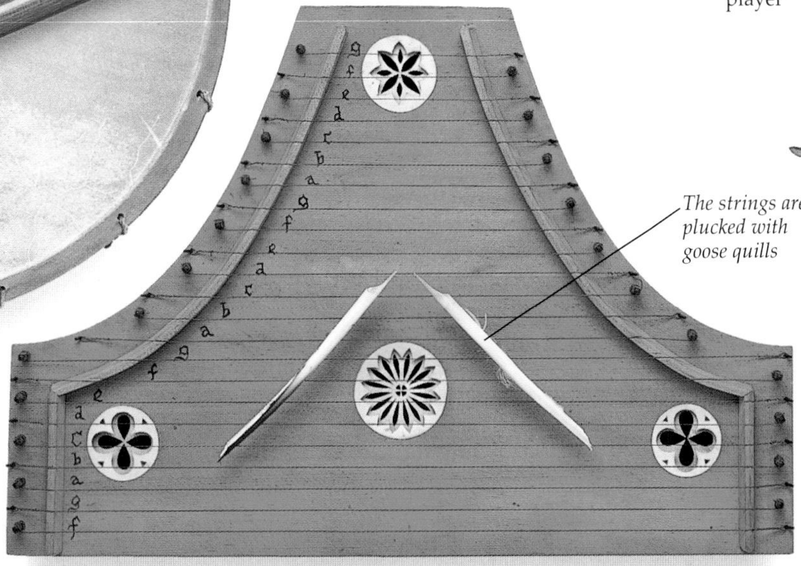

Bagpipes player

Sound comes out through pipes

The strings are plucked with goose quills

'Snare' adds a buzz to the sound of the tabor

HEAVENLY MUSIC
In medieval paintings, angels were often shown playing the psaltery. Similar to a small harp, it often formed part of a small orchestra, played with other soft instruments such as the lute (p. 44), the viol, or the flute.

Musician blows into mouthpiece to inflate the bag

Pipe is played with fingers

Pegs can be tightened to tune the strings

Outside strings are bass strings, or drones

Keys operate the two inside strings

Keys fall back into place by gravity

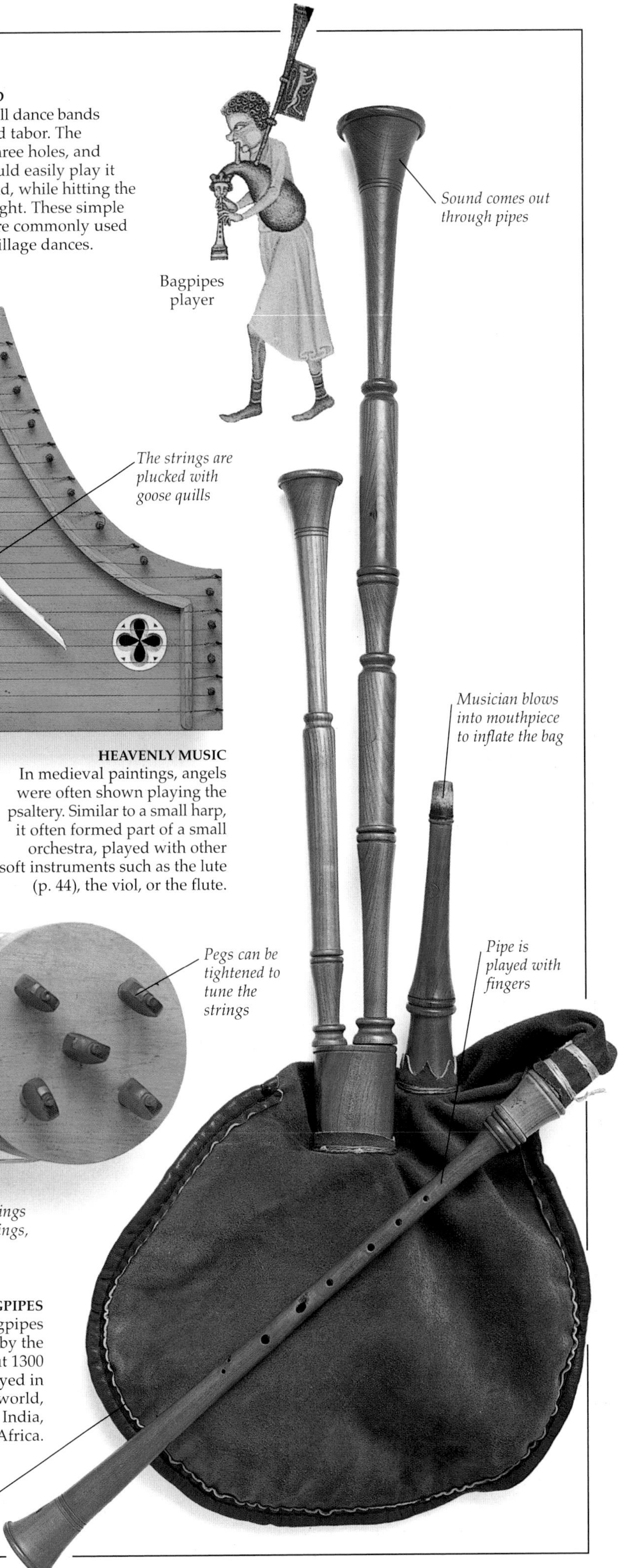

BAGPIPES
Contrary to legend, bagpipes were not invented by the Scots. In fact, in about 1300 they were being played in many parts of the world, including England, India, and North Africa.

Bag is made of leather

Plays and parades

MEDIEVAL DRAMA was started by the Church. Sometime in the 11th century, priests began to add short scenes to the major religious services, such as those at Christmas and Easter. The scenes portrayed the great moments in the bible – the fall of Adam, Noah escaping the flood, or Samson destroying the temple. People loved this new kind of entertainment. The scenes became so popular that they were performed in church porches, then on stages in town market places where more people could see them. By the 13th century, they had become complete cycles of plays, telling the whole Christian story and lasting as long as 40 days. In England, France, Italy, and Germany, they were staged by the local guilds (p. 50). They became known as "mystery" plays from the French word *metier*, or trade.

MASKS AND MUMMERS
Horses' heads, devil masks, drums, bells, and dances all played their part in a performance put on by mummers (above). On special occasions, mummers, or masked actors, staged short plays or mimes that told simple folk tales, usually featuring dramatic sword fights and a doctor, who would enter at the end of the story and bring the dead back to life.

WILD GREEN MEN
Many pagan (non-Christian) rituals lived on in medieval Europe. Bands of "wodwos", or wild woodmen, dressed in leaves and greenery would rush into feasts and pageants, causing havoc. Their dances symbolized the untamed forces of Nature. On the occasion shown above, their costumes accidentally caught fire from a candle!

The dragon can be made to "breathe" fire and smoke from its mouth by exploding small amounts of gunpowder inside its head

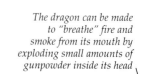

FESTIVAL FANFARE
The shawm was a reed instrument with a loud, piercing sound that was played at town parades and festivals.

FUNNY FACE
In 1230, a priest complained of actors who "change and distort their bodies with shameful leaps and gestures". This stone carving shows a fool or jester literally "pulling a face" to amuse his audience. Fools also entertained people by telling rude jokes and waving a pig's bladder filled with dried peas.

PLAYING THE DEVIL
Like church carvings and stained glass windows (pp. 34–35), mystery plays were a way of teaching the bible stories to ordinary people who could not read and write. In this scene, the Devil is seen tempting Jesus in the wilderness. Each section of a mystery play was mounted on a wagon and drawn to a series of stations throughout the town. If spectators waited long enough in one spot, they would see the whole cycle of plays.

Carved wooden head decorated with bright paint

SNAP DRAGON
This wooden head belonged to a parade dragon that was used in processions to celebrate the feast day of St George in the town of Norwich, England. It was operated by a man hidden inside the basketwork body and caused great amusement by snapping at the people who lined the streets. Dragons also played an important part in many mummers' plays, where they were usually shown battling with the valiant St George.

The back of the dragon's head was fitted with a long wooden pole which was used for manoeuvring the head

Lower jaw can be pulled up to make a snapping noise

Death and disease

DEATH WAS EVER-PRESENT for people living in the Middle Ages. Medical knowledge was limited and the average life expectancy was about 30 years. Frequent wars and famines claimed thousands of lives at a time, and disease was rife in the dirty, overcrowded streets of medieval towns and cities. The most catastrophic event of all was the Black Death. Carried by black rats, it was brought back from Asia by Italian sailors. The plague was deadly and highly contagious. Symptoms included black and blue blotches on the body and no cure was ever found. It swept through Europe between 1347 and 1350. By the end of 1348, at least a third of the entire population of Europe had died.

FEVERFEW
Strong-smelling feverfew was used to treat headaches and to assist in childbirth.

MARJORAM
Marjoram was used to make healing poultices to place on bruises and swellings.

LEMON BALM
This plant was seen as a kind of magic elixir that could cure serious illnesses. It was also used for fevers and colds because it causes sweating.

LUNGWORT
Because the shape of its leaves resembled lungs, lungwort was used to treat chest disorders.

HERBAL MEDICINE
Medieval medicine was based mainly on folklore and superstition rather than scientific observation. For example, many medical handbooks recommended that healing herbs should be picked on magical days of the year, such as Midsummer's Eve. However, many of the herbs in use in medieval times are still employed by herbalists today.

Priest anoints a dying man with holy oil

DOCTOR'S SURGERY
The most common form of surgery was blood-letting (above), which was carried out by uneducated barber-surgeons. People believed it restored the balance of the body's fluids, but more often, it seriously weakened sick patients.

LAST RITES
People in the Middle Ages believed it was important to die properly. If they did not make a final confession of their sins to a priest, they thought that they would go to hell (p. 31). But as the Black Death raged, so many priests perished that most of the people who died were buried without prayers or ceremony.

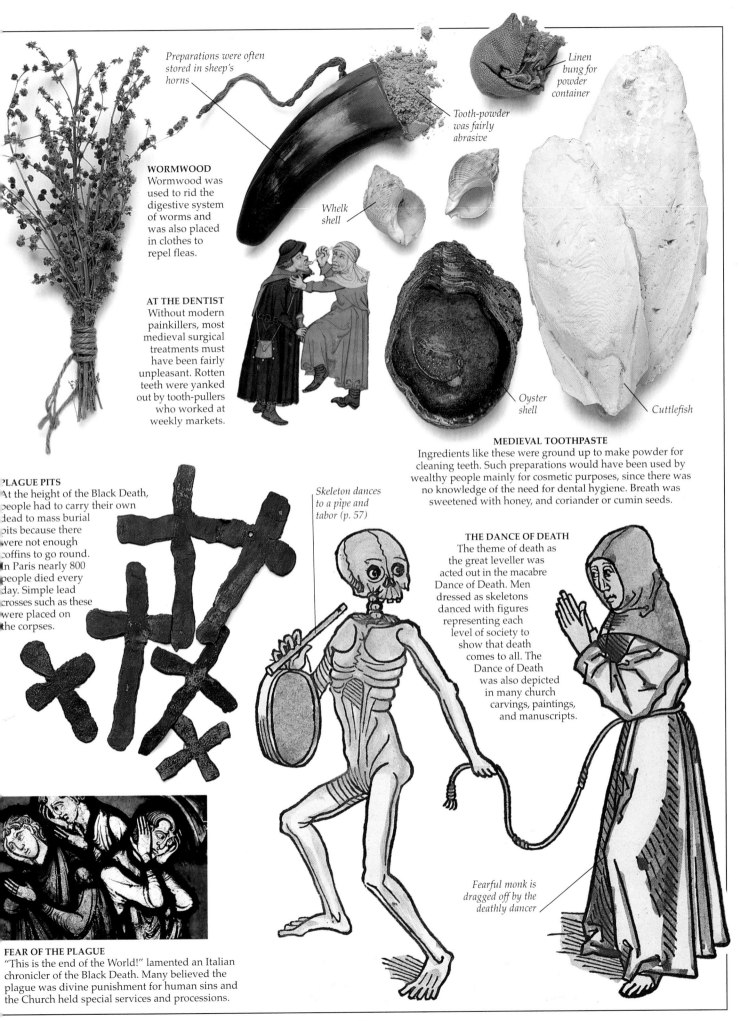

Preparations were often stored in sheep's horns

Linen bung for powder container

Tooth-powder was fairly abrasive

WORMWOOD
Wormwood was used to rid the digestive system of worms and was also placed in clothes to repel fleas.

Whelk shell

AT THE DENTIST
Without modern painkillers, most medieval surgical treatments must have been fairly unpleasant. Rotten teeth were yanked out by tooth-pullers who worked at weekly markets.

Oyster shell

Cuttlefish

MEDIEVAL TOOTHPASTE
Ingredients like these were ground up to make powder for cleaning teeth. Such preparations would have been used by wealthy people mainly for cosmetic purposes, since there was no knowledge of the need for dental hygiene. Breath was sweetened with honey, and coriander or cumin seeds.

PLAGUE PITS
At the height of the Black Death, people had to carry their own dead to mass burial pits because there were not enough coffins to go round. In Paris nearly 800 people died every day. Simple lead crosses such as these were placed on the corpses.

Skeleton dances to a pipe and tabor (p. 57)

THE DANCE OF DEATH
The theme of death as the great leveller was acted out in the macabre Dance of Death. Men dressed as skeletons danced with figures representing each level of society to show that death comes to all. The Dance of Death was also depicted in many church carvings, paintings, and manuscripts.

Fearful monk is dragged off by the deathly dancer

FEAR OF THE PLAGUE
"This is the end of the World!" lamented an Italian chronicler of the Black Death. Many believed the plague was divine punishment for human sins and the Church held special services and processions.

The birth of a new age

In the 15th century, there was a rebirth, or renaissance, of interest in the arts and sciences which began in Italy. The works of the great Latin and Greek writers were rediscovered and studied for the first time since the fall of Rome. They inspired artists and scholars to turn away from a strictly religious view of life and concentrate on human beings. Renaissance painters and sculptors began to explore the beauty of the human body, and poets wrote about human feelings and experiences. These new ideas also caused people to question traditional views on religion. Many thought that the Catholic Church (pp. 30–31) had become corrupt and needed change. A group of reformers called the Protestants rejected the authority of the Pope in Rome and set up new churches in northern Europe. This movement became known as the Reformation. It divided the Christian world and brought to an end the all-encompassing power of the medieval Church.

RELIGIOUS REFORMER
The religious Reformation was spearheaded by a German priest called Martin Luther (1483–1546). In 1517, he wrote a list of 95 arguments against Roman Catholic practices and nailed them to the door of Wittenberg Cathedral, provoking a wave of protest against the Church.

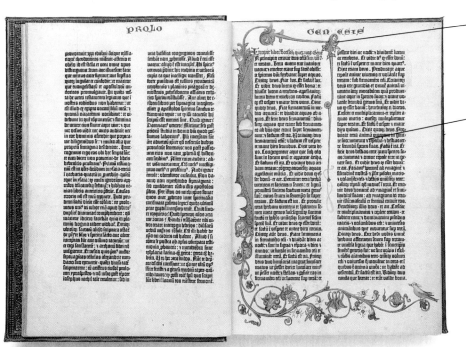

Hand-painted decoration

Gothic type imitates hand-written text

THE PRINTED WORD
Few inventions have changed the world as dramatically as printing with metal type. Printing was developed in Europe by Johannes Gutenberg (c. 1398–1468) who produced the first printed bible in the 1450s. This process replaced copying laboriously by hand, which made books rare and expensive.

PATRON OF PAINTERS
The Italian city of Florence was at the centre of the artistic Renaissance. This was due largely to men such as Lorenzo de' Medici (1449–1492). Nicknamed "the Magnificent", he used his wealth to employ artists such as Michelangelo (p. 7).

NEW SCHOOLS
Before the Renaissance, nearly all schools were run by the Church. Afterwards, many new grammar schools were founded by rich merchants and noblemen. The spread of education was hastened by the wider availability of books.

CONSTANTINOPLE FALLS
The Middle Ages ended as they began, with the invaders from the East. This time it was the Ottoman Turks. In 1453, after a long siege, they conquered Constantinople, which became the Muslim city of Istanbul. It was the end of the thousand-year-old Christian Byzantine Empire in the East (p. 6).

RENAISSANCE MAN
Leonardo da Vinci (1452–1519) embodied the spirit of the Renaissance. He was a brilliant painter and sculptor who also had a keen interest in science, engineering, and architecture. His most famous painting is the *Mona Lisa*, but he also produced detailed anatomical drawings and sketches for numerous inventions, such as this flying machine.

NEW FIRE POWER
The development of guns made an enormous difference to warfare after the mid-14th century. Cannons could break down stone walls bringing an end to the era of the impenetrable castle.

THE GREAT NAVIGATORS
In the 15th century, Europeans embarked on great voyages of discovery as they searched for sea routes to Asia. From the 1420s, Portuguese sailors ventured down the long west coast of Africa in caravels like this one. In 1488, Bartholomew Diaz rounded the Cape of Good Hope and sailed into the Indian Ocean for the first time. By 1498, Vasco da Gama had reached India. Meanwhile, Christopher Columbus crossed the Atlantic in 1492 and claimed America for the Spanish king.

Did you know?

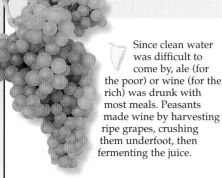

Town market in autumn, after a painting by medieval artist Jörg Breu the elder

Since clean water was difficult to come by, ale (for the poor) or wine (for the rich) was drunk with most meals. Peasants made wine by harvesting ripe grapes, crushing them underfoot, then fermenting the juice.

Although wealthy people imported carpets from the East during the Middle Ages, the carpets were too precious to be laid on the floor. Instead, they were draped over tables.

The walls of grand houses were hung with tapestries, heavy fabrics and leather panels, which added colour to the rooms, provided insulation against the cold and displayed the family's wealth.

Textiles were an important part of a rich man's bed: most beds consisted of a rudimentary timber frame hung with opulent drapes that were intended as much to reflect status as to afford privacy and warmth.

Seating in early medieval homes consisted mainly of benches built along the walls. At a time when violence was widespread, people had to make sure nobody could sneak up behind them.

Blacksmiths played a central role in medieval society since they manufactured and mended every object made of metal, from chains, nails, tools, pots, locks, hinges and handles to weapons, wagon fittings and horseshoes.

Horseshoe

Peasants were required to hand over some of their produce to the lord of their manor. In addition, they had to give ten per cent of everything they grew to the village priest; this was called a tithe.

Medieval men and women usually slept in the nude, even in winter; one documented marriage contract from the thirteenth century even forbade a wife from wearing nightclothes without her husband's consent.

Late medieval beds were warmed with long-handled brass pans filled with burning embers from the fire. Occasionally, these pans were also used for smuggling healthy babies into noble ladies' chambers to replace still-born heirs.

Rich people in the Middle Ages wore sumptuous – frequently woollen – clothes; individual garments were sometimes stored in smelly toilets, however, to discourage moths.

In larger houses, animals were often stabled on the ground floor so their body heat would rise up through the timber floorboards and help to warm the main rooms.

Another common source of heat was the brazier, a freestanding basket or pot – sometimes on a stand – in which charcoal or coal was burned. Convenient and portable, braziers could also be dangerous, since burning charcoal gives off carbon monoxide.

Early fireplaces were commonly adorned with images inspired by nature. The one in Queen Eleanor's thirteenth-century chamber at Westminster displayed a figure of Winter with a "sad countenance" and "miserable contortions of the body".

The right to hold a weekly market could only be granted to a town by the king in a document called a charter. Since markets brought trade and prosperity to a growing community, such a charter was of vital importance.

Infants' cradles were frequently made from birch wood, which was believed to repel evil spirits. (Elder, in contrast, was thought to attract them.)

Slender, shapely legs were considered very masculine in medieval times: to show them off, fashionable men wore close-fitting trousers or short trousers with woollen hose.

Tight boots accentuated calves

Henry VII coin

Q Was the structure of a royal court during the medieval era as formal and complex as popular mythology suggests?

A In our less regimented age, it's difficult to imagine the rigid and intricate hierarchy that surrounded medieval kings and queens. The bed of Henry VII of England, for example, required a retinue of attendants just to maintain it: there was a gentleman usher to draw the curtains, a groom to carry in fresh straw regularly for the mattress, a squire and yeoman to tie, lay and test it for concealed weapons, cover it with canvas, a feather bed (like a duvet) and perfumed sheets and blankets, and a special squire of the body to anoint the bed with holy water. Any necessary textile repairs were made by designated sewers, curtains were changed by more lowly staff called yeoman hangers, and running maintenance was undertaken by similarly humble, but often quite specialized, personnel.

Q How did the criminal justice system work during the Middle Ages?

A The local lord would settle disputes within his own manor and decide on the most suitable punishment for each crime. Some offenders would be executed, others would be fined, and those who had committed minor misdemeanours were likely to be sentenced to a period in the stocks or pillories: timber contraptions fitted with holes in which a captive's ankles (stocks) or wrists and head (pillories) would be locked. These devices were set up in public places, and as part of the punishment, passers-by were encouraged to throw rotten fruit. On the whole, only military and political prisoners were shut away, usually within a large castle.

French book illustration from about 1206 showing townspeople taunting a woman in the pillories

Q How safe were the streets of a medieval town?

A During the day, with the bustle of the crowds and markets, the most common dangers came from pickpockets and dishonest traders. After the sun went down, though, the pitch-dark streets harboured robbers and violent criminals. At dusk, therefore, bells were rung to sound the curfew – the time when, by law, everybody had to be indoors. After this time, nightwatchmen patrolled the streets with candle lanterns to discourage villains and catch anyone who was out after curfew.

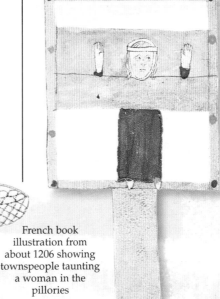

Record Breakers

UNBROKEN LINK
With the exception of Edward V and Edward VIII (who were never crowned), every British monarch since 1066 has been crowned in Westminster Abbey, in London. The original building, consecrated in 1065, was later demolished, but was largely rebuilt by 1272, and finally completed during the eighteenth century.

LONDON BRIDGE IS GOING UP
The first stone bridge across the River Thames in London was commissioned by Henry II in 1170 and was completed in 1206, after he died. With its drawbridge, double row of houses and 140 shops, it soon became one of the world's most famous bridges, and remained the only stone Thames bridge until 1750.

DEADLY ENEMY
The biggest killer ever to hit Europe, the Black Death (bubonic plague) wiped out 25 million people – one third of the total population – in the three years between 1347 and 1350.

POTENT SYMBOL
One of the most durable product symbols in history has its origins in medieval times. Beers and ales of the day, just like their modern equivalents, varied widely in strength, so their containers were labelled accordingly: "X" for the weakest, up to "XXXX" for the most potent. In 1924, an Australian brewery revived the "XXXX" symbol, which is still widely advertised and recognized today.

Westminster Abbey, London, England

Who's who?

Richard the Lionheart

THE FEUDAL TERRITORIES OF MEDIEVAL EUROPE were totally dominated by those who held land, power and money: the kings, emperors and nobles. A smaller group of people – rebels and revolutionaries – dedicated their lives to changing the status quo. Observing and recording the times they lived in, artists, writers and scientists produced work that helped to spread knowledge, enrich spirits, and enhance our modern historical understanding.

POWER AND NOBILITY

Charlemagne

CHARLEMAGNE (742–814)
King of the Franks (early inhabitants of France), Charlemagne united much of modern France and Germany. A great leader and law-maker and a champion of arts and letters as well as a legendary warrior, he was crowned first Holy Roman Emperor by Pope Leo III.

ALFRED THE GREAT (c846–899)
Initially King of Wessex, Alfred made peace with the Viking leader Guthrum under the Treaty of Wedmore and assumed control of all England. As ruler, he reformed Saxon law, promoted education and commissioned the *Anglo-Saxon Chronicle*, a history of the English people.

KING CNUT (CANUTE) (c994–1035)
When the Viking Svein Forkbeard died in 1014, his son Cnut inherited his Danish crown but was challenged to his father's English throne. After two years of conflict, however, Cnut triumphed, becoming the respected king of an empire that was soon to include Norway and southern Sweden as well as Denmark and England.

WILLIAM THE CONQUEROR (c1027–1087)
Aggrieved that the English throne went to Harold, Earl of Wessex, when it had been pledged to him by Edward the Confessor, William invaded England in 1066 and defeated Harold at the Battle of Hastings. As king, he brought stability and introduced the feudal system.

FREDERICK I (BARBAROSSA) (c1121–1190)
Holy Roman Emperor from 1152, Frederick I (his nickname means "red beard") unified the German states. He drowned crossing a river on his way to the Third Crusade.

HENRY II (1133–1189)
Only 21 when he became English king, Henry Plantagenet was involved in reforming the Church. Lord of an empire that also included much of France, he also laid the foundation for common law, including the right to trial by jury. (*see also* St Thomas Becket)

SALADIN (1137–1193)
Egyptian sultan who recaptured Jerusalem from the Crusaders. Defeated elsewhere by Richard I, he agreed the right of Christians to undertake pilgrimages to the Holy City.

RICHARD I (1157–1199)
Known as "the Lionheart", Richard ruled for 10 years, most of which he spent at war in France and on the Third Crusade. One of England's most celebrated kings, he passed just seven months of his reign at home.

PHILIP II (1165–1223)
Ruler of France from 1180, Philip, also known as Philip Augustus, fought three English kings – Henry II, Richard I and John – to gain control of their French territories, a goal he finally accomplished in 1214.

KING JOHN (1166–1216)
Younger brother of Richard I, John is remembered mainly as the signatory of Magna Carta (Great Charter): its limiting of royal power was a milestone in English constitutional history.

FREDERICK II (1194–1250)
Holy Roman Emperor from 1212, Frederick led the Sixth Crusade, returning Jerusalem temporarily to Christian rule. A religious sceptic, he was considered the most cultured man of his time.

LOUIS IV (1214–1270)
Outstandingly moral and brave king of France, Louis was revered across Europe and fought in two Crusades. He died of the plague on his way to lead the Eighth Crusade, and he was later canonized.

PHILIP VI (1293–1350)
Philip was the first French king of the house of Valois, which was based in the province of Burgundy. Inherited in 1328, his crown was challenged by Edward III of England, who defeated him in battle at Crécy in 1346. Edward later surrendered his claim in return for French territories.

EDWARD III (1312–1377)
English ruler and instigator (in 1337) of the 100 Years' War in support of his claim to the French throne. Edward was also responsible for major legal and parliamentary reform at home. His son, also called Edward, was a great soldier known as the Black Prince from the colour of his armour.

Edward the Confessor

HENRY V (1387–1422)
Inheriting the English throne in 1413, Henry redoubled the war against France and defeated the French at Agincourt in 1415. By 1420, he had established himself as the French heir, but he died before he could succeed, and all his conquests were lost in the reign of his son Henry VI. (*see also* Joan of Arc)

VLAD TEPES (c1430–1476)
Romanian baron who murdered thousands of people by impaling them on stakes, earning him the nickname "Vlad the Impaler". His unparalleled cruelty provided the basis of the Dracula legend.

REBELLION AND REFORMATION

St Francis of Assisi

ST BENEDICT (c480–c550)
Founder of the Benedictine religious order and creator of its vows of poverty, chastity and obedience. Known as "St Benedict's Rule", these vows were eventually adopted by holy orders across Europe.

ST THOMAS BECKET (1118–1170)
Henry II's Archbishop of Canterbury and close friend, Becket quarrelled with the King about Church reform. As a result, four of Henry's knights murdered him, and he was later canonized.

ST FRANCIS OF ASSISI (c1182–1226)
A rich man who gave his fortune away, Francis founded the Franciscan order of friars, who travelled around preaching, begging for food and communing with nature and animals.

SIMON DE MONTFORT (c1208–1265)
Organizer of a group of English barons who challenged King Henry III to reform his government – a council the King could consult at will. Defeating Henry in 1264, de Montfort summoned the first English Parliament, which included knights from each shire and citizens from the major cities and towns.

WAT TYLER (DIED 1381)
Leader of the English peasant revolt of 1381. King Richard II initially agreed to their demands to abolish high rents, serfdom and the poll tax, but he later recanted. During the fighting, Wat Tyler was killed by the Mayor of London.

JOAN OF ARC (1412–1431)
Peasant girl who led the French armies against the English forces of Henry VI. She was captured by the enemy and burned at the stake in Rouen, France, in 1431.

SAVONAROLA (1452–1498)
Italian friar, orator and reformer who led a revolt in Florence, Italy, that expelled the powerful Medici family and then established a republic. He also denounced the corrupt Pope, Alexander VI, who had him tortured and burned for heresy.

Joan of Arc (from a book illustration)

ARTS AND SCIENCES

ST BEDE (VENERABLE BEDE) (c673–735)
English monk and scholar who wrote, among other important works, the *Ecclesiastical History of the English Nation*, a primary source for students of English history. He also produced a history of the saints, a study of holy martyrs and a textbook to help his pupils write poetry in Latin.

AVICENNA (c980–1037)
Arabian philosopher and physician whose *Canon Medicinae* (*Canon of Medicine*) combined his own knowledge with that of Roman and Arabic physicians to become the standard work for centuries.

GIOTTO (c1267–1337)
Born in Florence, Italy, Giotto di Bondone founded the central tradition of western painting and had an enormous influence on Renaissance artists such as Masaccio and Michelangelo.

Geoffrey Chaucer

GEOFFREY CHAUCER (c1340–1400)
One of the greatest poets of the Middle Ages, Chaucer is best known for his *Canterbury Tales*, a collection of stories told by pilgrims on their way to Thomas Becket's shrine in Canterbury.

CHRISTINE DE PISAN (1364–1429)
One of the few medieval women to write books and poetry professionally (at this time, few women could even read and write), Christine de Pisan often dealt with feminist issues.

JOHANNES GUTENBERG (c1398–1468)
German inventor of printing using movable metal type arranged in words and lines, instead of the solid printing blocks for each page that were used previously. Gutenberg printed two early versions of the bible.

JAN VAN EYCK (DIED 1441)
Born in the Netherlands, Jan van Eyck is one of the most revered of all early painters. Although much of his youthful history is uncertain, his mastery of colour and detail left an unequalled model for his successors throughout the Renaissance and beyond. They also left us with a unique insight into the quality of medieval life.

Johannes Gutenberg (in blue) in his workshop

Find out more

BECAUSE MOST EXISTING MEDIEVAL BUILDINGS are imposing monuments, such as castles or cathedrals, rather than domestic dwellings, they don't give us much idea about what everyday life was like when they were built. Also, because the Middle Ages are so far removed – and so different – from our own time, it takes a lot more learning and imagination to create a mental picture of this time than it does to imagine the more recent past.

Ways you can find out more about the medieval world include looking at websites and other illustrated books and, if possible, visiting museums or visitor attractions that attempt to conjure up the atmosphere of life hundreds of years ago. One such attraction is Bede's World in north-eastern England. It focuses on the life and times of the Venerable Bede, a monk who lived 1,300 years ago (see page 67). The complex includes a museum and a recreated medieval village with an experimental farm that has three large buildings constructed in the way they would have been in St Bede's day.

HE WELCOMES A YOUNG MAN CALLED BEDE TO THE MONASTERY

VENERABLE BEDE
In this medieval-style icon created in the twenty-first century by Peter Murphy, Bede is welcomed to the monastery by his patron Benedict Biscop (pronounced Bishop). Biscop was a local nobleman and intellectual whose travels to Rome inspired him to create the enlightened atmosphere in which Bede flourished.

Modern Northumberland cross in eighth-century style

ANCIENT FARM
The demonstration farm at Bede's World was once a derelict fuel-storage site. Its reconstructed buildings are based on medieval examples excavated locally, while the crops and animals are all bred to resemble primitive stock as closely as possible: the dexter cattle in the foreground, for example, are smaller than most modern breeds.

Heraldic colours repeated on shield

Some surcoats had short sleeves

MODERN TOURNAMENTS
In many countries, medieval societies stage authentic re-enactments of large-scale battles or tournaments. At this mock fifteenth-century skirmish at Goodrich Castle in England, two knights in full body armour wear distinctive surcoats that bear the heraldic motif of their respective lords.

ABBEY OF MONT-ST-MICHEL, FRANCE
The community of Benedictine monks who still live in this medieval Abbey take all their meals in this lofty, sunlit refectory, near the building's highest level (see background image). The simple life they lead here carries on traditions that were first established by St Benedict during the tenth century.

BURIAL TREASURE
Discovered in a burial mound excavated at Sutton Hoo, Suffolk, England in 1939, this spectacular iron helmet is thought to have belonged to a local ruler during the seventh century. The helmet, along with other objects from Sutton Hoo, is on display at the British Museum.

Helmet trimmed with gold

ANCIENT RITUALS
In some Christian churches, censers, or incense burners, are swung from side to side to disperse a rich, smoky fragrance during services. In medieval times, rituals involving incense were an important part of worship in the Catholic Church, which dominated society.

Censer suspended from gilt chains

Places to visit

BEDE'S WORLD, JARROW, UK
Set up in and around the church and the site of the monastery where Bede lived, the complex features:
- a permanent exhibition, *The Age of Bede*, which explores and explains his world
- living-history displays that include early genetic strains of farm animals, early species of vegetables and grains and the tools and techniques used to cultivate them

ABBEY OF MONT-ST-MICHEL, NORMANDY, FRANCE
With parts dating back to the eleventh century, this fortified abbey (which still houses Benedictine monks), occupies one of the most dramatic locations in France. Visitors can see:
- the monk's refectory, with its rows of soaring windows
- the abbot's lodgings where he entertained important guests

CORSA DEL PALIO, SIENA, ITALY
Celebrated on July 2 and August 16 in the heart of Tuscany, this medieval festival offers:
- a bareback horse race first recorded in 1283
- stunning displays of costumes, flags and general pageantry

LUBECK, NORTHERN GERMANY
An important Baltic town during the Middle Ages, Lubeck still has many original features from that time. Among them are:
- the Holstentor, once the only gate into the city, built during the fifteenth century
- The Dom, a fantastic cathedral begun in 1173 and completed in 1230

BRITISH MUSEUM, LONDON, UK
In addition to precious works of art and jewellery from the Middle Ages, the British Museum also displays:
- artefacts discovered in a barrow excavated in Sutton Hoo, Suffolk, in 1939, including weapons, buckets and a musical instrument
- a gilt copper and enamel altar cross dating from about 1160

METROPOLITAN MUSEUM OF ART, NEW YORK, USA
Although "the Met" displays some of its rich medieval collection in the main building on Fifth Avenue, most of it is at The Cloisters in north Manhattan. The museum's only branch, it was constructed during the 1930s from fragments of medieval architecture brought back from Europe. Worth seeing are:
- the life-sized tomb effigy of a thirteenth-century crusader
- the apse from a twelfth-century Spanish church, which contains 3,000 limestone blocks
- the deck of fifteenth-century playing cards adorned with hunting images and symbols

Twelfth-century casket adorned with scenes of Thomas Becket's murder

Glossary

ARTISAN Skilled craftsman such as a metalworker, carpenter or stone mason.

BARON Highest-ranking noble; barons received their fief directly from the monarch. (*see also* FIEF)

BISHOP Powerful church official, equal in status to a baron. Each bishop ruled over a large administrative area called a diocese, controlling all the priests and monasteries within it.

BUTTERY Room where food and drink are prepared and stored.

BUTTRESS Stone or brick mass built against the external walls of a large building, such as a cathedral, to give additional strength. Buttresses are usually positioned at points of stress caused by roofs, arches or vaults.

CHAMLET Early cloth woven from wool and goat's hair that was widely used for everyday garments.

CORDWAINER Medieval term for shoemaker, from the city of Cordoba in Spain, which was associated with fine shoe leather.

COSTREL Small leather flask traditionally used by peasant farmers for carrying ale into the fields.

COURTIER One of the officials and nobles who served the monarch at court.

DAIS Raised platform at one end of a great hall, where the lord's table was positioned.

DAUB A mixture of clay, straw and dung plastered over wattle for insulation, forming a wattle-and-daub wall. (*see also* WATTLE)

DEMESNE The land belonging directly to a lord (as opposed to his manor – the land controlled by him). (*see also* MANOR)

FALCONRY Practice of keeping and training falcons; in medieval times, falcons were mainly used for hunting.

Falconry

Fenestral window, Timoleague Abbey, Ireland

FALLOW Description of farm land left uncultivated so it can regain the nutrients used up by repeated planting.

FAST Period of abstinence from all or some types of food as a religious observance.

FENESTRAL WINDOW Type of window with a wooden frame. Over this was stretched resin-and-tallow-soaked linen, which let in light and reduced draughts.

FEUDAL SYSTEM System of land and power distribution based on the allocation of land in return for services.

FIEF Land that is held under the feudal system. (*see also* FEUDAL SYSTEM)

FREEHOLDER Person who owns his own land, as opposed to being allowed the use of it under the feudal system. (*see also* FEUDAL SYSTEM)

GARGOYLE Water spout carved in the form of a grotesque human or animal figure that projects from a roof, wall or tower.

GLEBE Village land belonging to a parish priest, where he grew his own food.

GUILD Company or association connected with a particular craft or skill, such as shoemaking, weaving or masonry. Many of the guilds established during the Middle Ages still exist today.

HABIT Distinctive robes worn by monks and nuns to indicate their vocation, and often their order.

HALL Principal and largest domestic space in a medieval palace or home, where family, officials and servants spent most of their time.

HERETIC Someone who expressed an opinion that contradicted church doctrine.

HIPPOCRAS Medieval drink made from wine mixed with honey and herbs.

Knight on horseback

JOUST Competition between two knights in which they ride towards each other, each trying to knock the other off his horse.

KNIGHT Nobly born and armoured warrior on horseback. Knights may serve a lord, or they may be lords themselves.

LANCET WINDOW Tall, slender window with a pointed arch at the top, very popular in the thirteenth century.

LEWIS Iron tool used for gripping heavy blocks of stone so they can be lifted.

Gargoyle

LORD Male knight or noble, often holder of a castle and estate that provide a living for his family, his servants and the peasants on his land.

MANOR Territory under the control of a lord: usually his house or castle, a village, a church and the surrounding land.

MANOR HOUSE The home of a lord and lady and the centre of community life. Manor houses, even if they weren't castles, were usually well fortified against attack.

MINSTREL Wandering performer during the Middle Ages who wrote and sang songs, played an instrument and wrote poetry.

MOOR Member of the Muslim ruling class in Spain during the Middle Ages.

MUMMER Actor, usually one of a travelling troupe that put on plays.

NOBLE Person belonging to the aristocracy by birth or rank; baron, knight, bishop, etc. (*see also* BARON, KNIGHT)

PEASANTS People who worked on a lord's estate in return for a small plot of land on which they could grow crops to feed themselves and their families.

PEDLAR Salesman who travels from place to place hawking an assortment of small, inexpensive items.

PEWTER Metal alloy (usually containing tin, lead and copper) widely used during the Middle Ages for things such as tableware, candlesticks and jewellery.

PILGRIM Someone who travelled to a sacred place as an act of religious devotion; such journeys were called pilgrimages.

PLAINSONG (PLAINCHANT) Style of unaccompanied chanting used by medieval monks to recite their sacred texts. Plainsong has a single melodic line that follows the rhythm of the words.

POTTAGE Thick soup or stew made from vegetables, grain and meat stock.

SCUTAGE Specific payment (also called shield money) payable by a vassal to his lord in lieu of military service.

SEEDLIP Small basket for seeds being sown by hand.

SERF Peasant labourer, also called a villein. Serfs virtually belonged to their lord, who allowed them a small piece of land on which to live and work in exchange for labour under the feudal system. (*see also* FEUDAL SYSTEM)

SHAWM Early reed instrument with a piercing sound (forerunner of the oboe) that was popular for parades and festivals.

SICKLE Handled implement with a curved blade used for harvesting crops or trimming growth.

SMITH Metal worker. A blacksmith works in iron, a goldsmith in gold, etc.

SOLAR Private room for a noble and his family, away from the largely communal spaces that dominated most castles and manor houses.

STOCKS Instrument of public punishment consisting of a wooden frame with holes for the prisoner's ankles. Passers-by were encouraged to jeer and throw rotten fruit. Pillories held a prisoner's neck and wrists in the same way.

STYLUS Writing implement used by medieval scholars to scratch letters onto wax tablets.

SURCOAT Tunic worn over a knight's armour, bearing the heraldic motif of his lord.

TITHE Ten per cent portion of everything a peasant produced that had to be given to the local priest.

TONSURE Style of shaving a monk's or priest's head, usually on the crown, to indicate his status.

TOURNAMENT Popular entertainment featuring mock skirmishes. As well as giving pleasure to the crowd, tournaments provided practise for real warfare.

Shawm

TOURNEY Mock battle staged as part of a tournament. (see also TOURNAMENT)

TRENCHER Thick slab of stale bread used as a plate. Having soaked up any gravy or juices, trenchers were either eaten by the diners themselves, given to the poor or fed to the animals.

TRENTAL Package of 30 masses (services) said on behalf of an individual or family in exchange for a large payment to the church.

TROUBADOUR Medieval poet/musician, especially one who specialized in ballads of courtly love.

TRUCKLE (TRUNDLE) BED Small bed that rolls out on wheels from under a larger one, used in medieval times to accommodate a child or servant.

VASSAL Someone who owes services to another person in return for land under the feudal system. (*see also* FEUDAL SYSTEM)

VILLEIN see SERF

Wattle-and-daub construction

VISOR Flap on the front of a helmet that can be pulled down to protect the face.

WASTEL Type of fine white bread eaten only by the rich. Poor people ate coarse wholewheat loaves.

WATTLE Interwoven branches used to form the basic structure of walls. (*see also* DAUB)

WIMPLE Headdress worn by medieval women (and still by some nuns). Wimples wound around the head, down over the ears and under the chin, falling in folds across the neck for maximum coverage.

WINDLASS Machine for hauling or lifting heavy objects (such as building blocks) using a wheel and axle.

WRIT Signed document, usually from a monarch or a high-ranking official, passing a law or granting permission for something.

Distinctive shaved head or tonsure

Medieval monk

A wimple is fastened to the hair with pins

Wimple

Index

Acknowledgements

Dorling Kindersley would like to thank:
The York Archaeological Trust for Excavation and Research Ltd; Richard Fitch and Mark Meltonville of Wolfbane; Peter and Joyce Butler, and Tracy Chadwick (medical herbalist) of Saxon Village Crafts; Anthony Barton, medieval musical instrument consultant; Bob Powell at the Weald and Downland Open Air Museum, Sussex; Steve Hollick and Chris Kemp, and all members of the National Guild of Stonemasons and Carvers, London; Caroline Benyon at Carl Edwards Studio; the Department of Medieval and Later Antiquities at the British Museum, London; the Museum of London; Jon Marrow at Norton Priory Museum Trust; the Dean and Chapter of York; All Saints Church, North Street, York; St Nicholas Church, Stanford-on-Avon; Castle Museum Norwich, Norfolk Museums Service; Susila Baybars for editorial help; Joe Hoyle and Cormac Jordan for design help.
Additional photography by Peter Anderson (40bc, 49cl, 52c,bl, 55c, 60tr, 61tr); John Chase (42cr, 46–47, 61cl); Andy Crawford (54bl); Steve Gorton (19tr, 32–33c); Peter Hayman, Ivor Kerslake, and Nick Nichols (22cr, 30c,l, 31bl, 42cl,bc); Gary Ombler (38–39)
Model by Peter Griffiths (32–33)
Artworks by Anna Ravenscroft (40);

John Woodcock (52–53)
Endpapers by David Graham

The publisher would like to thank the following for their kind permission to reproduce their photographs:
t=top b=bottom m=middle l=left r= right
AKG, London: 6br, 38bc, 61br, 62bl; 64tr; /Photo: Erich Lessing/San Apollinare in Classe, Ravenna: 6lc, /Photo: Erich Lessing /Galleria dell'Accademia, Florence: 7rc; /Pfarrkirche, Cappenberg: 7bl; /Nuremburg City Library: 19tl; /Bern, Burgerbibliotheque: 21tl; /Bibliothèque de St Genevieve: 31tl; /Bibliothèque Nationale, Paris: 48tr, 56tr, 61tc, 63tr; /Visioars 65mr; **The Art Archive:** /British Library 60tl; /Chiesa di San Francesco Pescia/Dagli Orti 67tl; /Musze Thomas Dobrze Nantes/Dagli Orti 67tr. **Ancient Art & Architecture Collection:** 25bl, 32tr; **Musée des Arts Decoratifs,** Paris/Photo: Sully-Jaulmes: 14c; **Ashmolean Museum, Oxford:** 7c, 45bl; **Avoncroft Museum of Historic Building:** 71tr; **Keith Barley:** 35tl; **Bede's World:** 68m, 68tl, 68bl; **Bridgeman Art Library, London:** /Bibliothèque de la Sorbonne, Paris: 6bl; /Trinity College, Dublin: 6tr; /British Library, London: 7tc, 9br, 10br, 10bl, 12br, 14cl, 15bl, 20tr, 22cl, 23cl, 24br, 30tl,

31tr, 36b &c, 42br, 43cl, 45cl, 50br, 50cl, 51cl, 54br, 58c, 60br, Front Jacket: lc & tl, Back Jacket: lac, bl, b, tc, rbc, Inside front flap; /With special authorisation of the City of Bayeux: 7tl; /Victoria & Albert Museum, London: 8tr; /Musée Condée, Chantilly; /Giraudon: 12tr, 17tr, 30bc, 60bl; /Vatican Library, Rome: 15tl; /Fitzwilliam Museum, University of Cambridge: 15cl, 27bl, Back Jacket: tc; /Bibliothèque Nationale, Paris: 22tr, 27tl, 28tr, 44tr, 45tc, 54c, Back Jacket: tr; /Kunsthistorisches Museum, Vienna: 24bc; /Department of the Environment, London: 25tl; /Westminster Abbey, London: 26tr; /Sixt Parish Church, Haut-Savoie, France: 31br; /Galleria degli Uffizi, Florence: 35br; /San Francesco Upper Church, Assisi: 37tl; /Seminario Patriarcale, Venice: 47bl; /Staatsarchiv, Hamburg: 47tc; /British Museum: 48bl; /Bibliothèque Royale de Belgique, Brussels: 48c; /City of Bristol Museum & Art Gallery: 62tl; /Bibliothèque de l'Institut de France, Paris /Giraudon: 63tl; **British Library, London:** 53br, 54cr, 54tl, 56c, 62c, 66-67, Front Jacket: bcr; **British Museum, London:** 27r, 30bl, 45tr, 69ml, 69m, 69br,

Back Jacket: lc; **Jean-Loup Charmet, Paris:** 41tl, 42tr; **Musée de Cluny, Paris:** 62c; **Corbis:** Bettmann 67br; **Danish National Museum, Copenhagen:** 6c; **The English Heritage Photo Library:** 68br; **E.T. Archive,**

London: 24ac, 29tc, 34tl; /Victoria & Albert Museum, London: 11br, 11cr, 16tl; /British Library, London: 14tr; /Biblioteca Marciana: 22bl; /Bibliothèque Nationale, Paris: 28bl; /Biblioteca Estense, Modena: 38c; /Collegio del Cambio, Perugia: 46cl; /Biblioteca Augustea, Perugia: 53tr; **Mary Evans Picture Library, London:** 24tr, 66mrb; /Institution of Civil Engineers: 66tr; **Werner Forman Archive, London;** /Metropolitan Museum of Art, New York: 45br; Photographie; Giraudon /Bibliothèque Nationale, Paris: 8tl; Sonia Halliday & Laura Lushington Photographs /Victoria & Albert Museum, London: 12c ; **Sonia Halliday Photographs:** 35c, 58tr; **Robert Harding Picture Library:** 7br, 26br, 33tl, 40br, 51tl, 56bl; **Michael Holford:** 14bl; **Museum of London:** 52bc; **Puffin Books: Churches & Cathedrals by Helen Leacroft, 1957. Reproduced by permission of Penguin Books Ltd:** 33tr, 33cr; **Scala, Florence:** /Archivo di Stato, Siena: 8lc; /Muséo dell'Opera del Duomo, Orvieto: 50tl, 50bl, 51br, 51tr; **Sir John Soane's Museum, London:** 33br, 70m; **Trinity College Library, Cambridge:** 39tr; **Wallace Collection:** 25tr, 49tl; **Woodmansterne:** 61bl; **Zefa Pictures:** 48br.
Jacket credits: All Saints Church back br, back c; Ashmolean back br; British Museum back cr, front tr; Museum of London back br; Wallace Collection front main image.